MathFlare

Name: _______________________

Class: ___________

Teacher: _______________________

Copyright © 2024 MathFlare Publishing.
All rights reserved. This book or any portion thereof may not be reproduced or used in any manner whatsoever without the express written permission of the publisher except for the use of brief quotations in a book review.

Introduction

As parents and educators, we recognize the pivotal role mathematics plays in shaping a child's academic journey and future success. Yet, the path to mathematical proficiency can often seem daunting, fraught with challenges and complexities. That's where the transformative power of MathFlare Workbooks shine through, illuminating the way forward with clarity, precision, and purpose.

Introducing MathFlare Workbooks – a beacon of guidance, a testament to excellence, and a catalyst for achievement. Crafted with meticulous care and expertise, MathFlare Workbooks stand as paragons of educational excellence, designed to nurture young minds, ignite a passion for learning, and develop a deep-rooted understanding of mathematical concepts.

Picture this: your child eagerly delves into the pages of Mathflare Workbook, greeted by a step-by-step guide illuminated with vivid examples that demystify complex mathematical concepts. With each turn of the page, they embark on a journey of discovery, encountering thoughtfully curated practice questions that reinforce learning and hone problem-solving skills. And when they unveil the answers to those very questions, a sense of accomplishment blossoms within them – a tangible reward for their hard work and dedication.

But MathFlare Workbooks are more than just tools for learning; they are pathways to comprehension, fostering a deep-seated understanding of mathematical concepts through a sequential, logical flow. From fundamental principles to advanced problem-solving strategies, every chapter builds upon the last, ensuring a robust foundation upon which future knowledge can be constructed.

As parents, we yearn for nothing more than to see our children thrive, to witness the spark of inspiration ignited within them as they conquer academic challenges with confidence and poise. MathFlare Workbooks serve as partners in this noble endeavor, offering not just practice questions, but the keys to unlocking a world of opportunity.

And for teachers, MathFlare Workbooks stand as invaluable allies in the quest to cultivate mathematical proficiency in the classroom. With answers readily available, instructors can focus on guiding and nurturing their students, confident in the knowledge that MathFlare Workbooks provide a solid framework upon which to build.

In the pages of MathFlare Workbooks, we find not just the promise of academic excellence, but the seeds of a brighter tomorrow. So let us embrace the power of mathematics, let us champion the journey of learning, and let us pave the way for a generation of young minds poised to shape the world. With MathFlare Workbooks as our guide, the possibilities are infinite, and the future, bright.

Table of Contents

MathFlare
MATH WORKBOOK
Grade 2
Step by Step Guide and Essential Practice with Answers
Addition Subtraction
Multiplication
Place Value and Expanded Notations
Geometry
MathFlare Publishing

MathFlare
MATH WORKBOOK
Grade 2-3
Step by Step Guide and Essential Practice with Answers
Addition Subtraction
Multiplication and Division
Place Value and Expanded Notations
Geometry
MathFlare Publishing

MathFlare
MATH WORKBOOK
Grade 3
Step by Step Guide and Essential Practice with Answers
Multiplication and Division
Decimals
Place Value and Expanded Notations
Fractions and Geometry

MathFlare
MATH WORKBOOK
Grade 1
Step by Step Guide and Essential Practice with Answers
Counting and Numbers
Addition and Subtraction
Place Value and Expanded Notations
Understanding Time
MathFlare Publishing

MathFlare
MATH WORKBOOK
Grade 1-2
Step by Step Guide and Essential Practice with Answers
Counting and Numbers
Addition and Subtraction
Place Value and Expanded Notations
Understanding Time
MathFlare Publishing

MathFlare
MATH WORKBOOK
Grade 3-4
Step by Step Guide and Essential Practice with Answers
Addition Subtraction
Multiplication Division
Place Value and Expanded Notations
Fractions and Geometry
MathFlare Publishing

MathFlare
MATH WORKBOOK
Grade 4
Step by Step Guide and Essential Practice with Answers
Addition Subtraction
Multiplication Division
Place Value and Expanded Notations
Fractions and Geometry
MathFlare Publishing

MathFlare
MATH WORKBOOK
Grade 4-5
Step by Step Guide and Essential Practice with Answers
Multiplication Division
Place Value and Expanded Notations
Fractions and Geometry
Unit Conversion
MathFlare Publishing

MathFlare
Grade 5
MATH WORKBOOK
Step by Step Guide and Essential Practice with Answers
Multiplication Division
Place Value and Expanded Notations
Fractions and Geometry
Unit Conversion
MathFlare Publishing

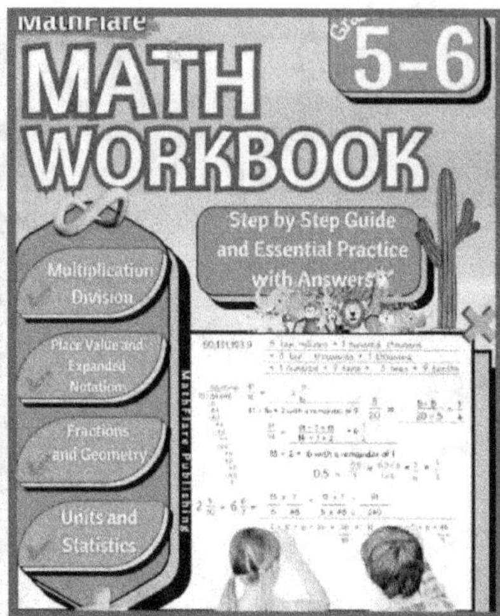
MathFlare
Grade 5-6
MATH WORKBOOK
Step by Step Guide and Essential Practice with Answers
Multiplication Division
Place Value and Expanded Notation
Fractions and Geometry
Units and Statistics
MathFlare Publishing

MathFlare
Grade 6
MATH WORKBOOK
Step by Step Guide and Essential Practice with Answers
Integers and Statistics
Arithmetic and Pre-Algebra
Fractions and Geometry
Ratio and Percentage
MathFlare Publishing

MathFlare
Grade 6-7
MATH WORKBOOK
Step by Step Guide and Essential Practice with Answers
Arithmetic and Pre-Algebra
Ratio, Percent Proportion
Geometry
Statistics
MathFlare Publishing

MathFlare
Grade 7
MATH WORKBOOK
Step by Step Guide and Essential Practice with Answers
Pre-Algebra
Ratio, Percent Proportion
Geometry
Statistics
MathFlare Publishing

MathFlare
Grade 7-8
MATH WORKBOOK
Step by Step Guide and Essential Practice with Answers
Pre-Algebra
Ratio, Percent Proportion
Geometry and Cartesian Plane
Statistics
MathFlare Publishing

MathFlare
Grade 8-9
MATH WORKBOOK
Step by Step Guide and Essential Practice with Answers
Pre-Algebra
Ratio, Proportion and Percentage
Linear Equations
Geometry and Cartesian Plane
MathFlare Publishing

MathFlare
Grade 8
MATH WORKBOOK
Step by Step Guide and Essential Practice with Answers
Pre-Algebra
Percentage
Linear Equations
Geometry
MathFlare Publishing

Roman Numerals

The table contains the list of roman numerals along with their Arabic number.

Roman Numeral	Arabic Number	Roman Numeral	Arabic Number	Roman Numeral	Arabic Number	Roman Numeral	Arabic Number
I	1	XI	11	XXI	21	XXXI	31
II	2	XII	12	XXII	22	XXXII	32
III	3	XIII	13	XXIII	23	XXXIII	33
IV	4	XIV	14	XXIV	24	XXXIV	34
V	5	XV	15	XXV	25	XXXV	35
VI	6	XVI	16	XXVI	26	XXXVI	36
VII	7	XVII	17	XXVII	27	XXXVII	37
VIII	8	XVIII	18	XXVIII	28	XXXVIII	38
IX	9	XIX	19	XXIX	29	XXXIX	39
X	10	XX	20	XXX	30	XL	40
XLI	41	L	50	LI	51	LXI	61
XLII	42	LI	52	LX	60	LXII	62
XLIII	43	LII	53	LXI	61	LXIII	63
XLIV	44	LIII	54	LXIV	64	LXIV	64
XLV	45	LIV	55	LXV	65	LXV	65
XLVI	46	LV	56	LXVI	66	LXVI	66
XLVII	47	LVI	57	LXVII	67	LXVII	67
XLVIII	48	LVII	58	LXVIII	68	LXVIII	68
XLIX	49	LVIII	59	LXIX	69	LXIX	69
L	50	LIX	59	LXX	70	LXX	70
LXXI	71	LXXX	80	LXXXI	81	XC	90
LXXII	72	LXXXI	81	LXXXII	82	XCI	91
LXXIII	73	LXXXII	82	LXXXIII	83	XCII	92
LXXIV	74	LXXXIII	83	LXXXIV	84	XCIII	93
LXXV	75	LXXXIV	84	LXXXV	85	XCIV	94
LXXVI	76	LXXXV	85	LXXXVI	86	XCV	95
LXXVII	77	LXXXVI	86	LXXXVII	87	XCVI	96
LXXVIII	78	LXXXVII	87	LXXXVIII	88	XCVII	97
LXXIX	79	LXXXVIII	88	LXXXIX	89	XCVIII	98
LXXX	80	LXXXIX	89	XC	90	XCIX	99
LXXXI	81	XC	90	XCI	91	C	100

Unit Conversion

Metric Conversion
1 meter (m) = 100 centimeters (cm)
1 meter (m) = 1000 millimeters (mm)
1 kilometer (km) = 1000 meters (m)
1 hectare (ha) = 10000 square meters (m^2)
1 square meter (m^2) = 10000 square centimeters (cm^2)
1 cubic meter (m^3) = 1000 liters (L)

Weights and Measures
1 kilogram (kg) = 1000 grams (g)
1 liter (L) = 1000 milliliters (mL)
1 tonne (t) = 1000 kilograms (kg)
1 centimeter (cm) = 10 millimeters (mm)
1 gram (g) = 1000 milligrams (mg)
1 kilometer (km) = 100000 centimeters (cm)

Geometry

Area and Perimeter

The area of a shape represents the amount of space it occupies. The perimeter of a shape is the total distance around its outer edge.

Area of Rectangle

For a square, since all four sides are equal, we only need to know the length of one side to find its area. We can calculate the area of a square by multiplying the length of one side by itself (squared). So, if the length of one side of the square is 's', then the area (A) is given by:

$A = s \times s$

4 in

4 in

$A = 4 \times 4$

$A = 16$

Perimeter of Rectangle

For a square, since all four sides are equal, we can find the perimeter by adding up the lengths of all four sides. If 's' represents the length of one side, then the perimeter (P) is given by:

$$P = 4 \times s$$

$$P = 4 \times 4$$

$$P = 16$$

Area of Triangle:

The area of a triangle represents the amount of space enclosed within its three sides. The formula for calculating the area of a triangle depends on the type of triangle. For a general triangle, we use the formula:

$$A = \frac{1}{2} \times base \times height$$

Where:

- *A* represents the area of the triangle.

- The base is the length of any one side of the triangle.

- The height is the perpendicular distance from the base to the opposite vertex.

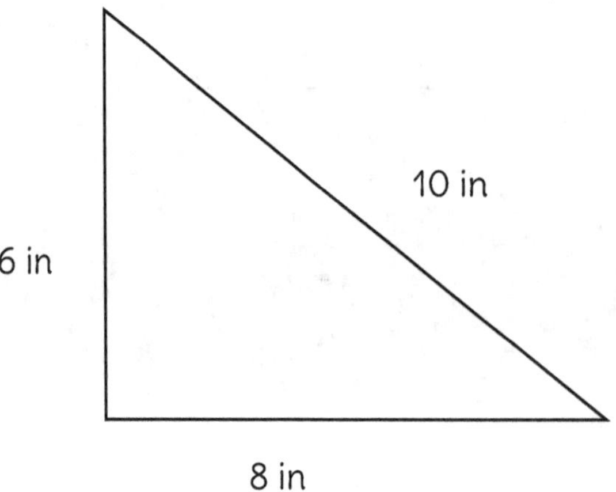

MathFlare - Units, Numerals, and Geometry

$$A = \frac{1}{2} \times \text{base} \times \text{height}$$

$$A = \frac{1}{2} \times 6 \times 8$$

$$A = \frac{1}{2} \times 48$$

$$A = 24$$

Perimeter of Triangle:

The perimeter of a triangle is the total length of its three sides. To find the perimeter, we simply add the lengths of all three sides together:

$$P = \text{side1} + \text{side2} + \text{side3}$$

$$P = 6 + 8 + 10$$

$$P = 24$$

Equilateral Triangle

An equilateral triangle is a triangle in which all three sides are equal in length. To find the area and perimeter of an equilateral triangle, we can use the following formulas:

- Area (A): $\frac{\sqrt{3}}{4} \times a^2$ where a is the length of one side of the equilateral triangle.

- Perimeter (P): $P = 3a$ where a is the length of one side of the equilateral triangle.

Let's solve a problem:

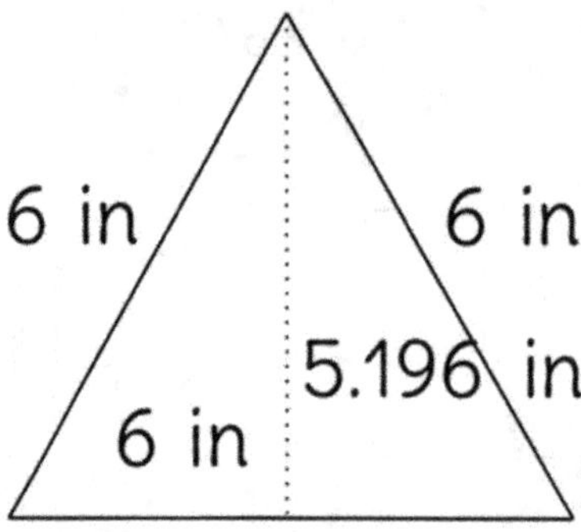

Area of Equilateral Triangle:

$$\text{Area (A)}: \frac{\sqrt{3}}{4} \times (6)^2$$

$$\text{Area (A)}: \frac{\sqrt{3}}{4} \times 36$$

$$\text{Area (A)}: \frac{36\sqrt{3}}{4}$$

$$\text{Area (A)}: \frac{36(1.73)}{4}$$

$$\text{Area (A)}: \frac{62.35}{4}$$

$$\text{Area (A)}: 15.59 \text{ in}^2$$

Perimeter of Equilateral Triangle:

$$P = 3a$$

$$P = 3(6) = 18$$

MathFlare - Units, Numerals, and Geometry

<u>Isosceles Triangle</u>

An isosceles triangle is a triangle with at least two sides of equal length. The angles opposite the equal sides are also equal.

Area of Isosceles Triangle

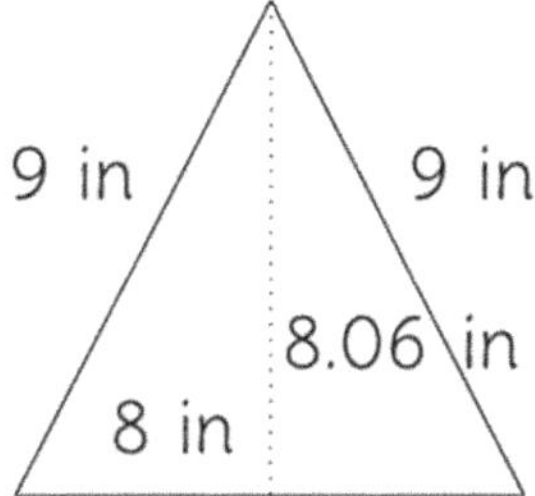

$$A = \frac{1}{2} \times base \times height$$

$$A = \frac{1}{2} \times 8 \times 8$$

$$A = \frac{1}{2} \times 64$$

$$A = 32$$

Perimeter of Isosceles Triangle

The perimeter of a triangle is the total length of its three sides. To find the perimeter, we simply add the lengths of all three sides together:

$$P = side1 + side2 + side3$$

$$P = 9 + 9 + 8$$

$$P = 26$$

Area and Circumference of circles

To find the area (A) and circumference (C) of a circle, we use the following formulas:

1. Area of a Circle (A) = $\pi \times (radius)^2$
   - where π (pi) is a constant with value of (3.14). It is a ratio of the circumference of a circle to its diameter,
   - the radius (r) is the distance from the center of the circle.
2. Circumference of a Circle (C) = $2 \times \pi \times radius$

Let's solve an example: suppose a swimming pool has a radius of 11 meters, we are required to calculate its Area and Circumference:

$$\text{Area } (A) = \pi \times (radius)^2$$

$$A = 3.14 \times 11^2$$

$$A = 3.14 \times 121$$

$$A = 379.94 \text{ square meters}$$

$$\text{Circumference } (C) = 2 \times \pi \times radius$$

$$C = 2 \times 3.14 \times 11$$

$$C = 69.08 \text{ square meters}$$

Angles

Types of Angles: Angles can be classified based on their measures:

- Acute Angle: An angle less than 90°.

- Right Angle: An angle exactly equal to 90°.

- Obtuse Angle: An angle greater than 90° and less than 180°.

- Straight Angle: An angle exactly equal to 180°.

- **Reflex Angle:** An angle greater than 180° and less than 360°.

- **Full Angle:** An angle equal to 360°.

Measure angles with a protractor. It looks like a semicircle or a half-disc with degree markings from 0° to 180°. To measure an angle using a protractor, we place the center of the protractor at the vertex of the angle, align one side of the angle with the zero mark on the protractor, and read the degree measure where the other side intersects the protractor.

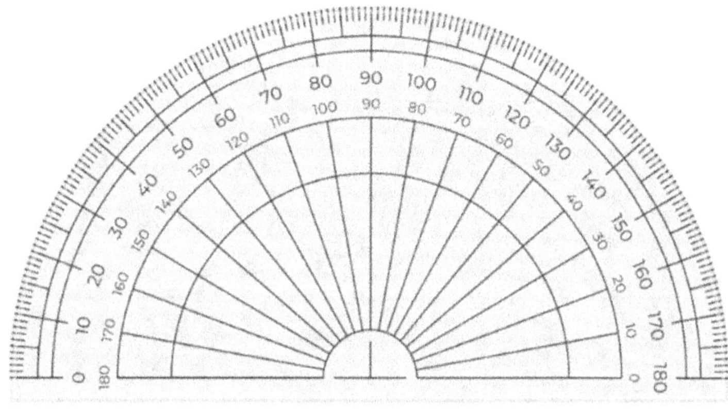

Image: Protector

For example, let's measure the following angle.

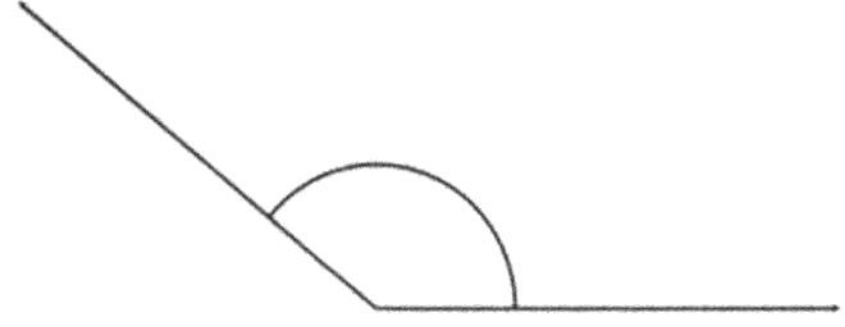

The angle is 140°.

We also know that the angle is greater than 90° and less than 180°, so this is an Obtuse angle.

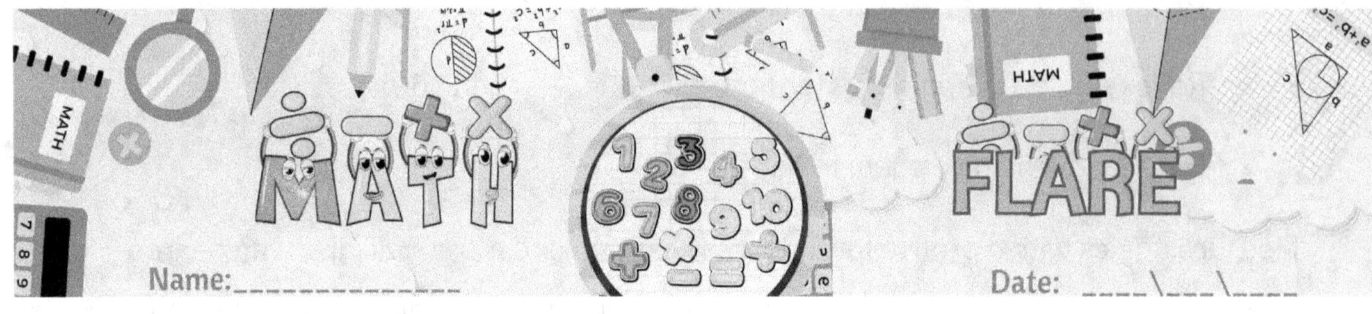

Roman Numerals

1. VII = __________________

2. 6 = __________________

3. 36 = __________________

4. XXXI = __________________

5. 339 = __________________

6. 71 = __________________

7. 68 = __________________

8. 87 = __________________

9. I = __________________

10. 73 = __________________

11. CDLXXXVII = __________

12. CDLXV = ______________

13. CXLVIII = ____________

14. CCCXI = ______________

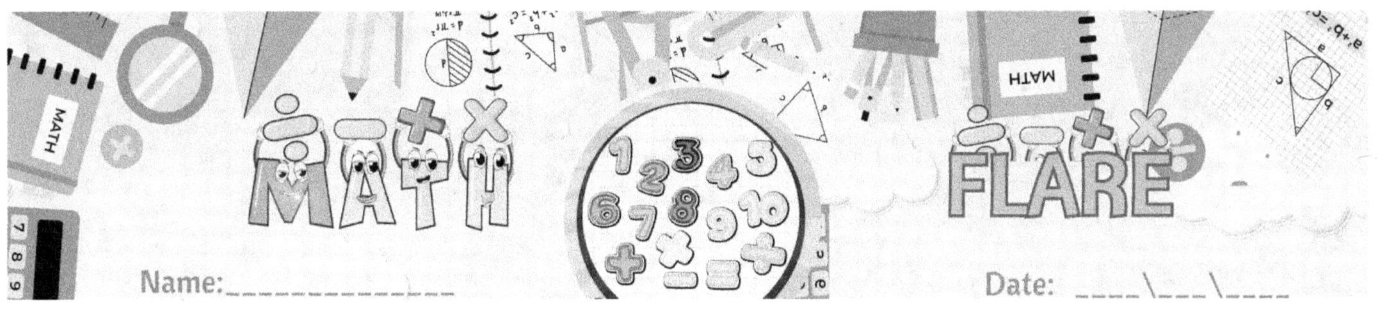

15. II = _______________

16. XLVII = _______________

17. IV = _______________

18. LXIII = _______________

19. III = _______________

20. 27 = _______________

21. CCXLVI = _______________

22. 58 = _______________

23. 197 = _______________

24. CCCIV = _______________

25. 9 = _______________

26. XC = _______________

27. 473 = _______________

28. 49 = _______________

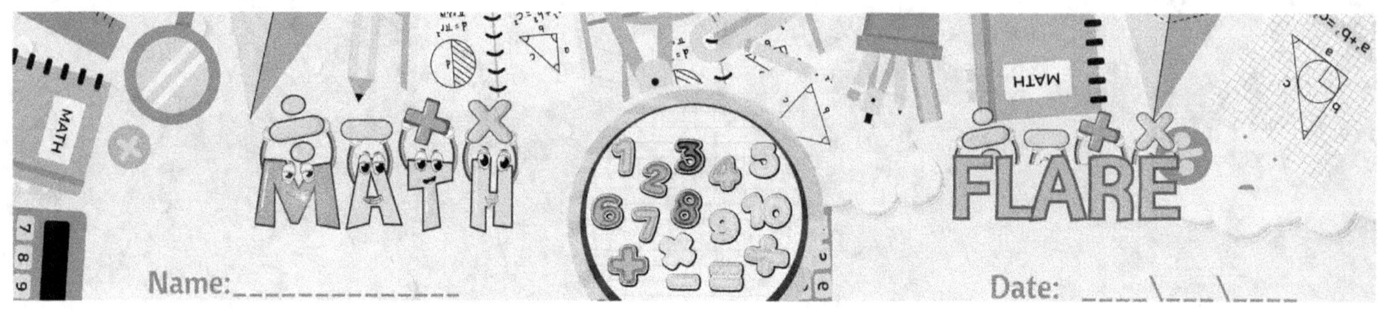

29. CDLXXX = _______________

30. 79 = _______________

31. 57 = _______________

32. LXXII = _______________

33. 99 = _______________

34. CXII = _______________

35. 237 = _______________

36. 395 = _______________

37. CCCLVIII = _______________

38. XIX = _______________

39. 273 = _______________

40. 217 = _______________

41. 39 = _______________

42. 409 = _______________

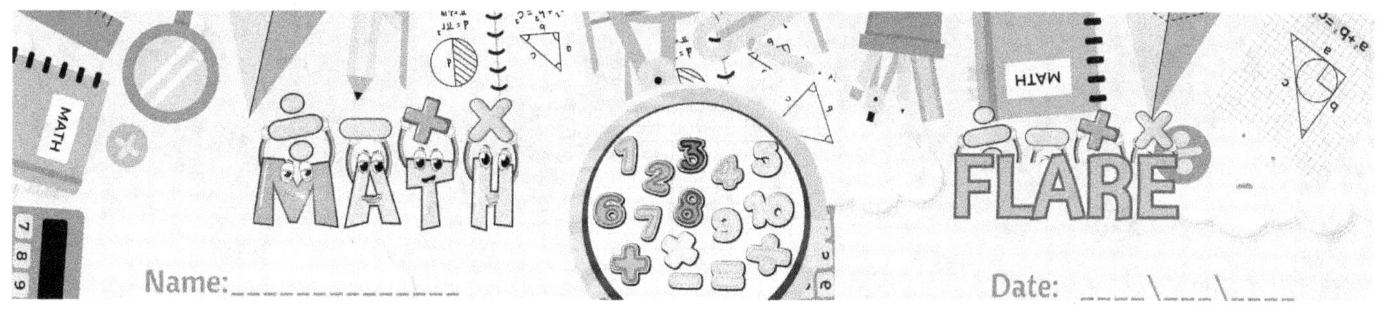

43. CCXLVIII = _____________

44. 10 = _____________

45. CCXXVII = _____________

46. 371 = _____________

47. 205 = _____________

48. LV = _____________

49. XXVIII = _____________

50. 80 = _____________

51. LXXXIII = _____________

52. LIV = _____________

53. XXIX = _____________

54. CDXXXVI = _____________

55. LXXIV = _____________

56. XXIII = _____________

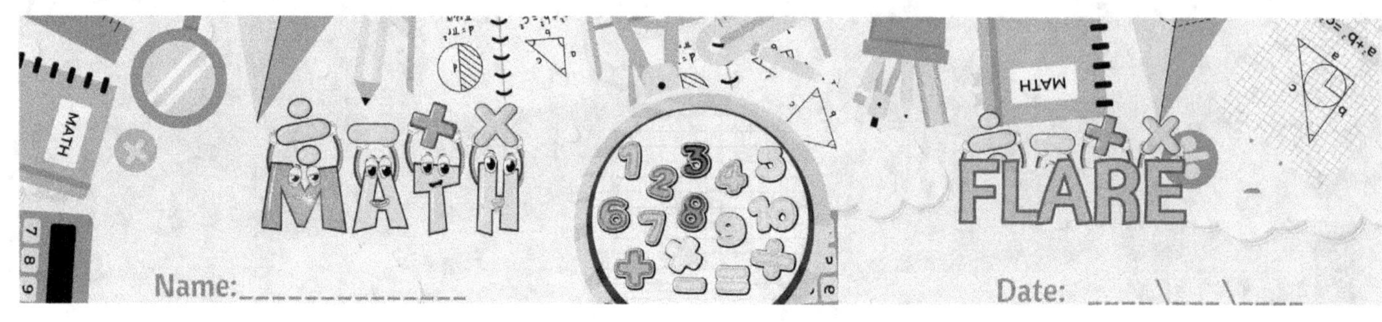

57. XVIII = _______________

58. CCLXXXIV = _______________

59. 65 = _______________

60. 256 = _______________

61. XLI = _______________

62. 130 = _______________

63. 331 = _______________

64. CCLVII = _______________

65. LVI = _______________

66. XIV = _______________

67. CCCXXV = _______________

68. 210 = _______________

69. 117 = _______________

70. 439 = _______________

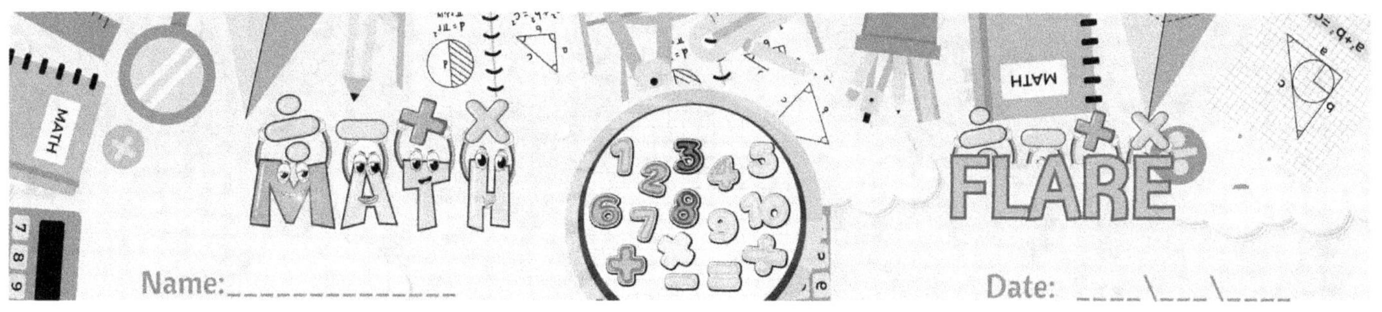

71. XCII = _______________

72. CDXV = _______________

73. CDLXXII = _______________

74. CCLXXII = _______________

75. CXLIX = _______________

76. 8 = _______________

77. 201 = _______________

78. 292 = _______________

79. XLV = _______________

80. V = _______________

81. 178 = _______________

82. 33 = _______________

83. CDLXXXV = _______________

84. 289 = _______________

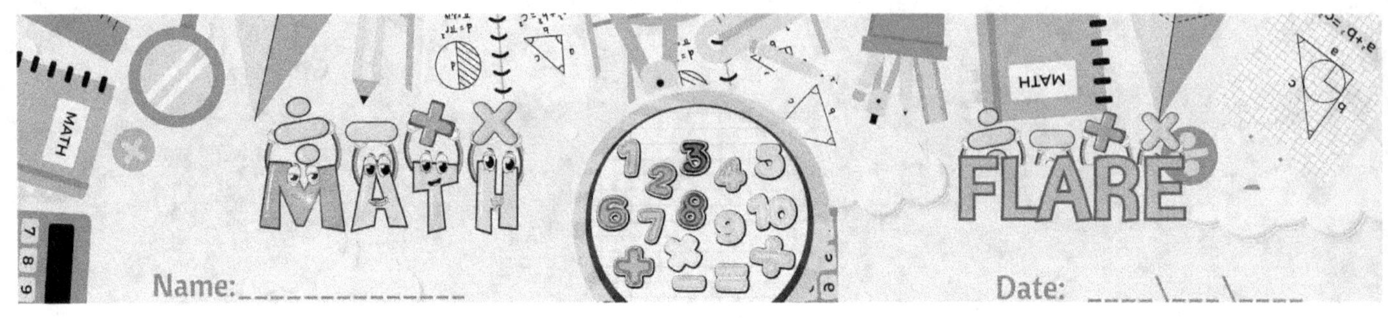

85. 345 = _______________

86. CCCVIII = _______________

87. CCLXX = _______________

88. 53 = _______________

89. CDLII = _______________

90. LXXXIX = _______________

91. XI = _______________

92. CCCXXXVIII = _______________

93. 81 = _______________

94. CCXI = _______________

95. 449 = _______________

96. 440 = _______________

97. 462 = _______________

98. 13 = _______________

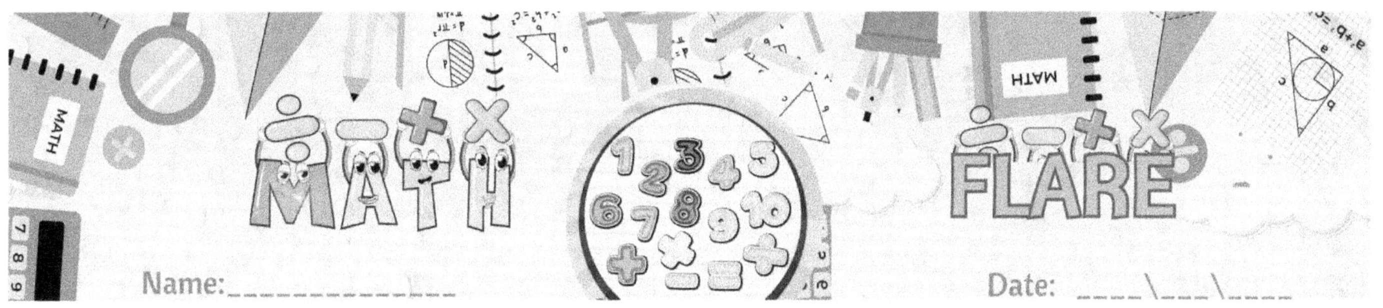

Name: _______________________ Date: ____________

99. 21 = _______________________

100. 403 = _______________________

101. CCCXIX = _______________________

102. 223 = _______________________

103. CCCXX = _______________________

104. 24 = _______________________

105. CDXC = _______________________

106. CCCLIV = _______________________

107. XLIV = _______________________

108. CDXCVIII = _______________________

109. XII = _______________________

110. 488 = _______________________

111. 429 = _______________________

112. 328 = _______________________

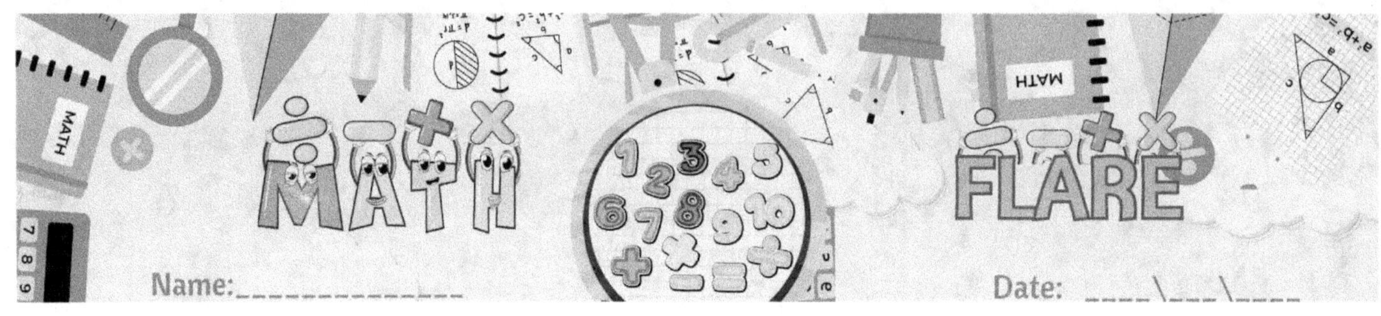

113. 258 = _______________

114. LXXXII = _______________

115. CCCVII = _______________

116. 166 = _______________

117. 52 = _______________

118. CCXII = _______________

119. 268 = _______________

120. CCCXXIII = _______________

121. CXXXVII = _______________

122. 295 = _______________

123. 76 = _______________

124. 454 = _______________

125. CCCXXIV = _______________

126. LXVI = _______________

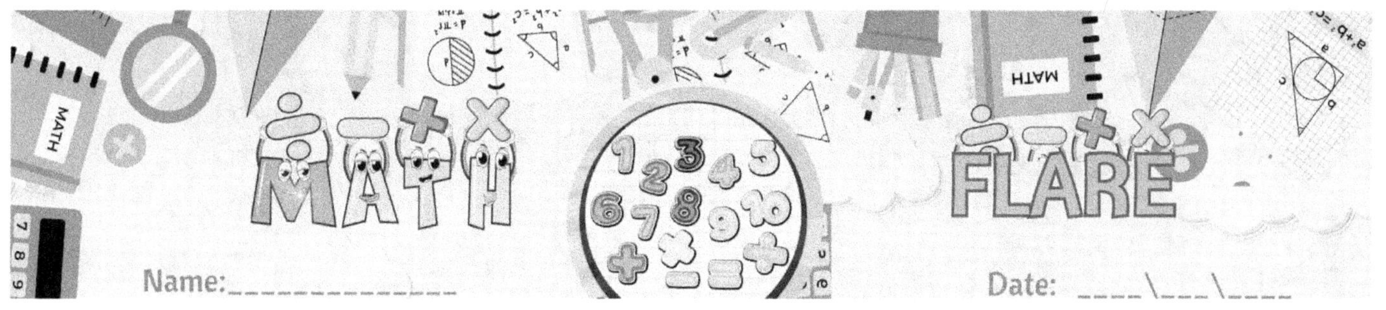

127. LXIX = _______________

128. XXVI = _______________

129. CDXXXVIII = _______________

130. LXXXIV = _______________

131. 42 = _______________

132. CDXLI = _______________

133. CCCLII = _______________

134. 492 = _______________

135. 310 = _______________

136. 152 = _______________

137. CCXL = _______________

138. 95 = _______________

139. CCCXXXIII = _______________

140. CCLXXVII = _______________

141. CXV = _______________

142. 456 = _______________

143. XXV = _______________

144. 381 = _______________

145. CDLXIX = _______________

146. 481 = _______________

147. LXXVII = _______________

148. LXXV = _______________

149. CXCIII = _______________

150. 260 = _______________

151. CCCV = _______________

152. 379 = _______________

153. 375 = _______________

154. 213 = _______________

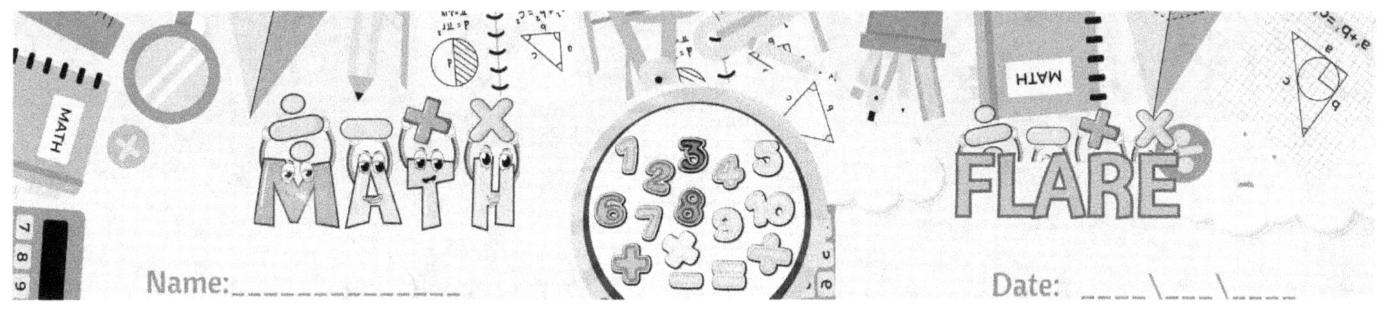

Metric Conversion

Convert the given measures.

155. 75 in = _______________ m

156. 37 ft = _______________ m

157. 76 in = _______________ m

158. 83 ft = _______________ m

159. 60 in = _______________ m

160. 31 ft = _______________ m

161. 86 ft = _______________ m

162. 90 ft = _______________ m

163. 84 ft = _______________ m

164. 11 in = _______________ m

165. 99 in = _______________ m

166. 73 in = _______________ m

167. 49 in = _______________ m

168. 13 ft = _______________ m

169. 63 ft = _______________ m

170. 29 ft = _______________ m

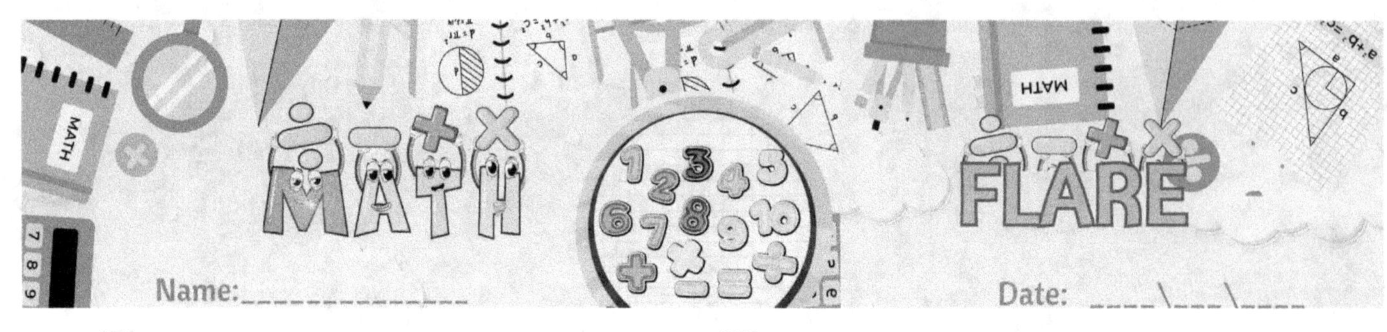

171. 59 in = _______________ m   172. 92 in = _______________ m

173. 10 in = _______________ m   174. 67 in = _______________ m

175. 91 in = _______________ m   176. 18 in = _______________ m

177. 71 ft = _______________ m   178. 37 ft = _______________ m

179. 37 ft = _______________ m   180. 25 in = _______________ m

181. 87 in = _______________ m   182. 22 in = _______________ m

183. 16 in = _______________ m   184. 37 ft = _______________ m

185. 25 ft = _______________ m   186. 71 in = _______________ m

187. 57 in = _______________ m   188. 61 in = _______________ m

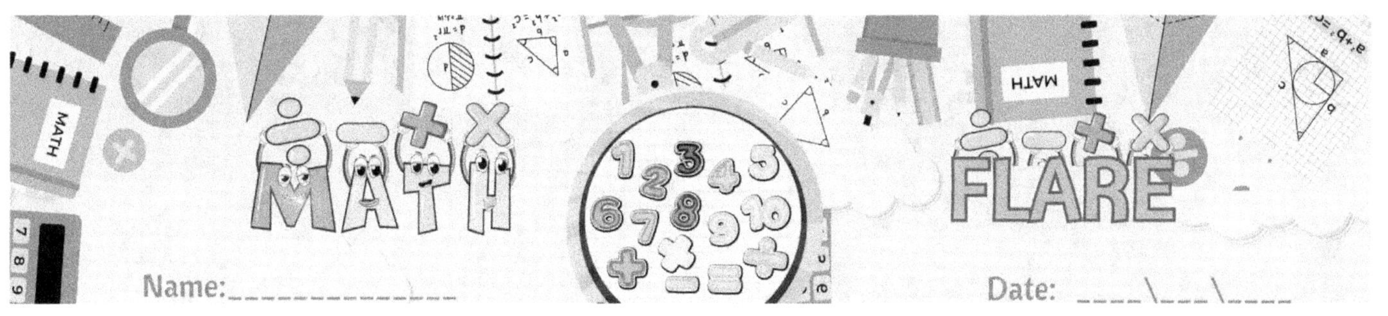

189. 92 ft = _____________ m

190. 59 in = _____________ m

191. 26 in = _____________ m

192. 41 ft = _____________ m

193. 18 ft = _____________ m

194. 92 in = _____________ m

195. 50 ft = _____________ m

196. 36 in = _____________ m

197. 25 ft = _____________ m

198. 29 ft = _____________ m

199. 62 in = _____________ m

200. 61 in = _____________ m

201. 56 in = _____________ m

202. 35 in = _____________ m

203. 69 ft = _____________ m

204. 85 in = _____________ m

205. 50 ft = _____________ m

206. 29 ft = _____________ m

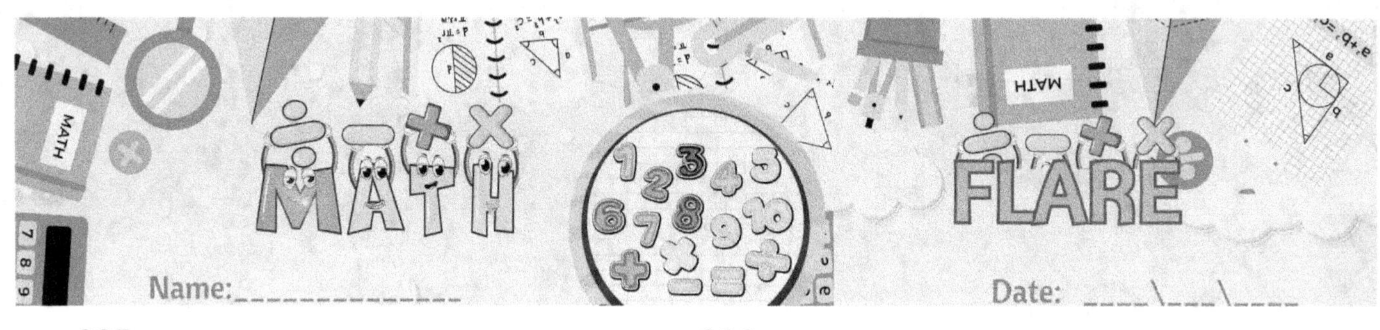

207. 84 in = _______________ m

208. 95 in = _______________ m

209. 64 in = _______________ m

210. 67 ft = _______________ m

211. 65 ft = _______________ m

212. 49 ft = _______________ m

213. 56 in = _______________ m

214. 45 ft = _______________ m

215. 43 in = _______________ m

216. 73 ft = _______________ m

217. 84 in = _______________ m

218. 56 in = _______________ m

219. 85 in = _______________ m

220. 38 ft = _______________ m

221. 25 ft = _______________ m

222. 87 in = _______________ m

223. 20 ft = _______________ m

224. 14 in = _______________ m

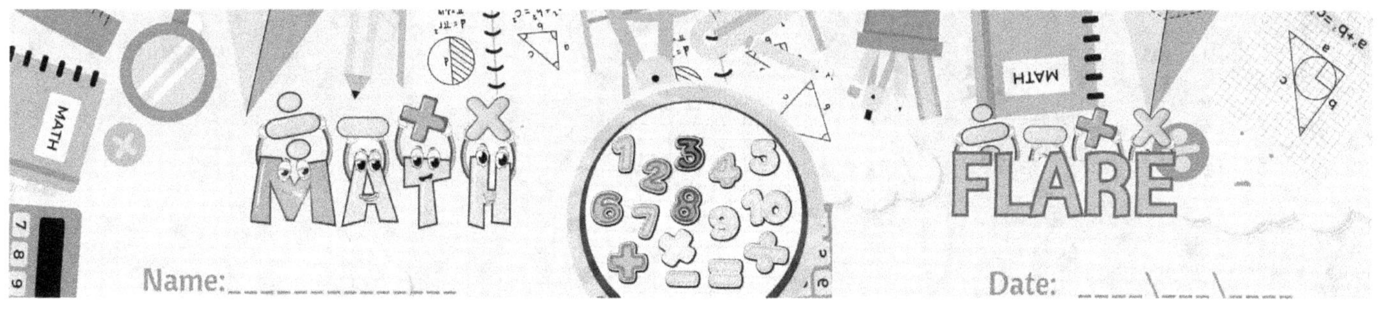

Name:________________   Date: ____________

Metric Weights and Measures

Convert the given measures to new units.

225. 14 m = ___________ cm   226. 28 g = ___________ t

227. 84 g = ___________ kg   228. 17 kg = ___________ t

229. 27 g = ___________ t   230. 65 m = ___________ cm

231. 92 km = ___________ cm   232. 52 kL = ___________ L

233. 75 mL = ___________ kL   234. 75 m = ___________ km

235. 68 t = ___________ kg   236. 62 km = ___________ cm

237. 31 L = ___________ mL   238. 87 km = ___________ cm

239. 95 t = ___________ g   240. 86 kL = ___________ mL

     16

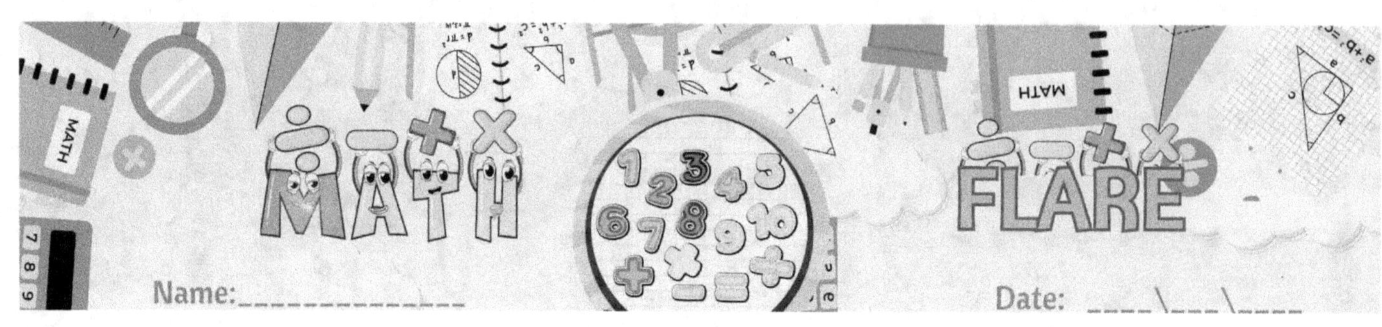

241. 61 L = _____________ mL

242. 97 kL = _____________ L

243. 35 L = _____________ mL

244. 93 km = _____________ m

245. 76 t = _____________ g

246. 84 t = _____________ g

247. 72 kL = _____________ L

248. 59 g = _____________ kg

249. 76 g = _____________ t

250. 52 cm = _____________ km

251. 68 mL = _____________ L

252. 43 t = _____________ kg

253. 34 km = _____________ m

254. 45 kg = _____________ t

255. 68 km = _____________ m

256. 25 t = _____________ kg

257. 65 kL = _____________ L

258. 81 L = _____________ kL

259. 31 km = _____________ m

260. 44 L = _____________ kL

261. 76 km = _____________ cm

262. 78 m = _____________ cm

263. 98 cm = _____________ m

264. 74 km = _____________ cm

265. 23 kL = _____________ mL

266. 73 mL = _____________ L

267. 79 km = _____________ cm

268. 76 mL = _____________ kL

269. 80 t = _____________ g

270. 31 cm = _____________ m

271. 63 kL = _____________ L

272. 69 t = _____________ kg

273. 90 L = _____________ kL

274. 50 m = _____________ km

275. 63 L = _____________ kL

276. 89 mL = _____________ L

Area and Perimeter: Rectangles and Triangles

277. 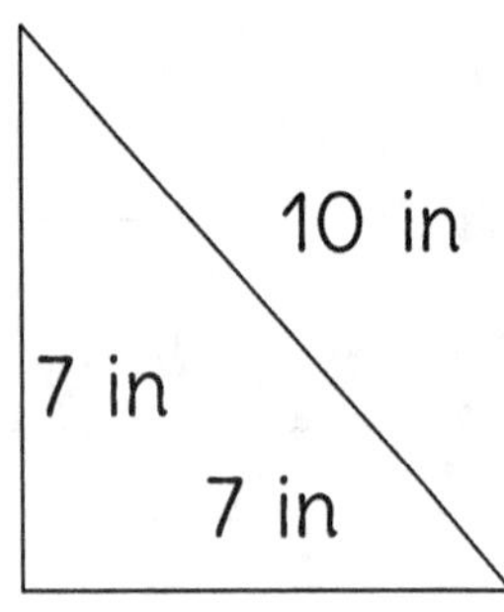

278. 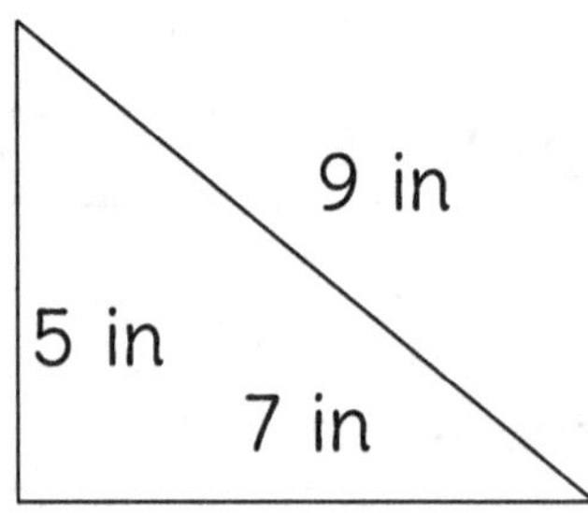

279. 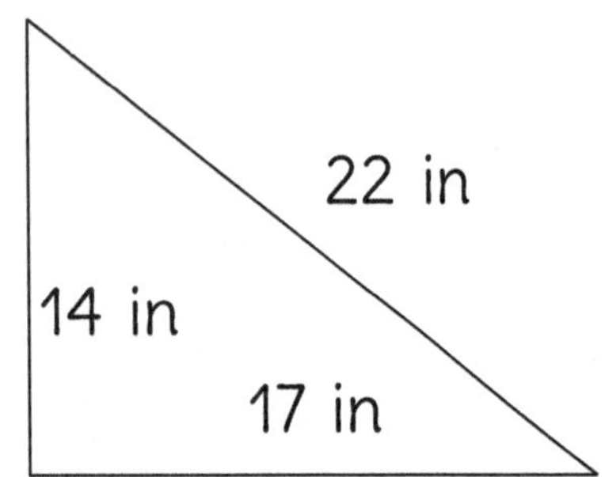

280. 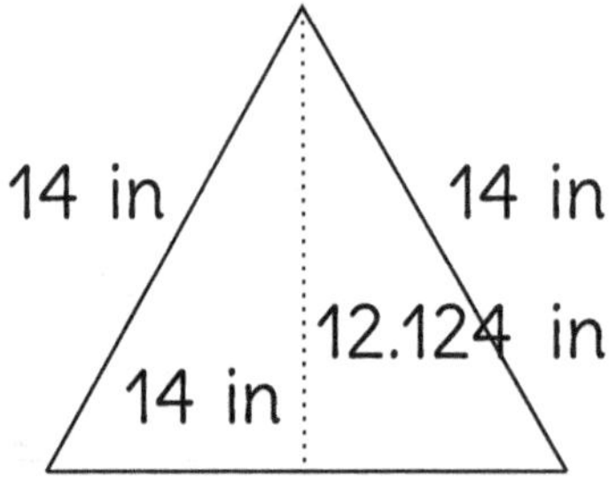

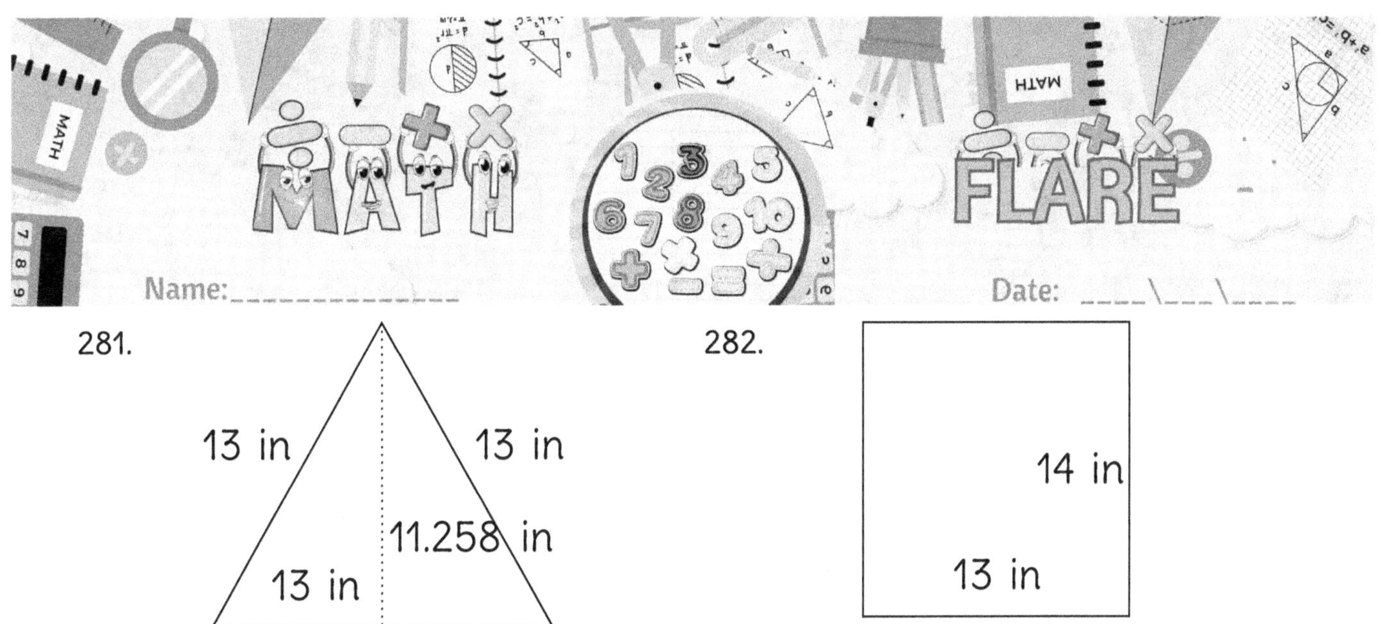

281.

13 in
13 in
13 in
11.258 in

282.

14 in
13 in

283.

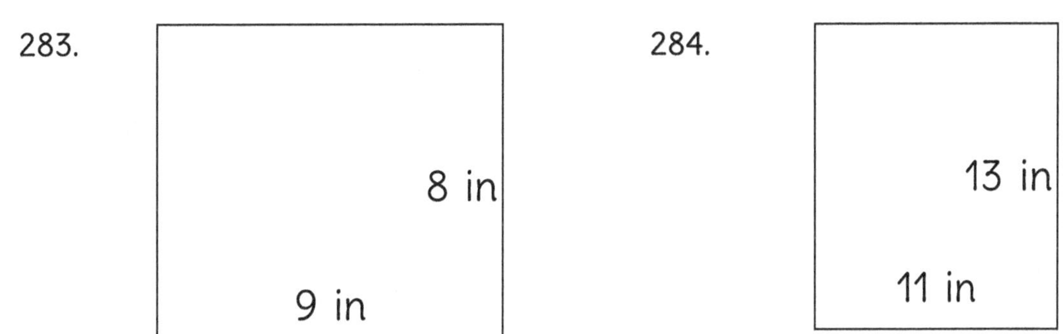

8 in
9 in

284.

13 in
11 in

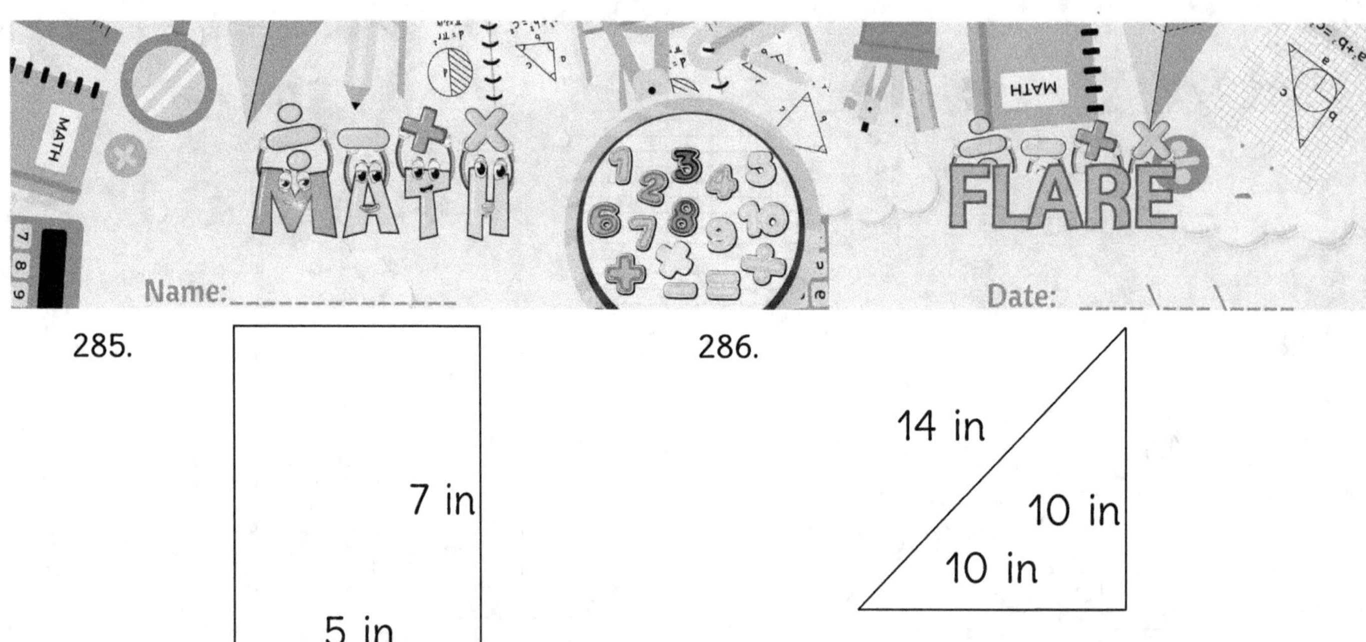

285.

7 in

5 in

286.

14 in

10 in

10 in

287.

9 in

9 in

7.794 in

9 in

288. 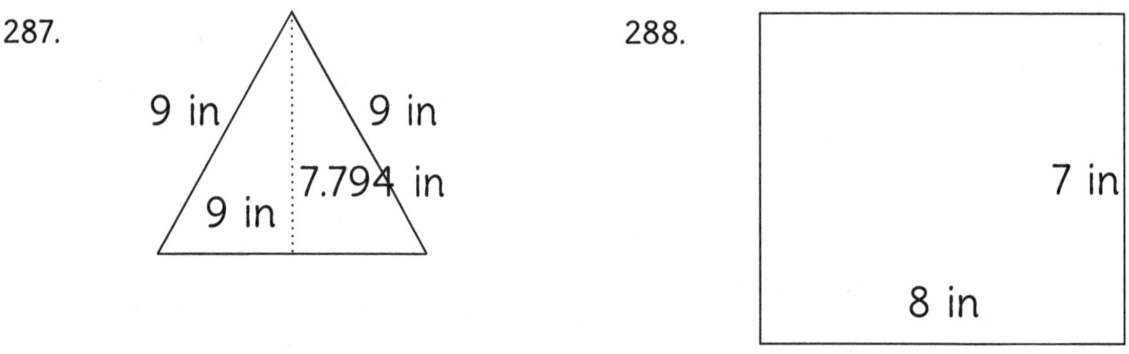

7 in

8 in

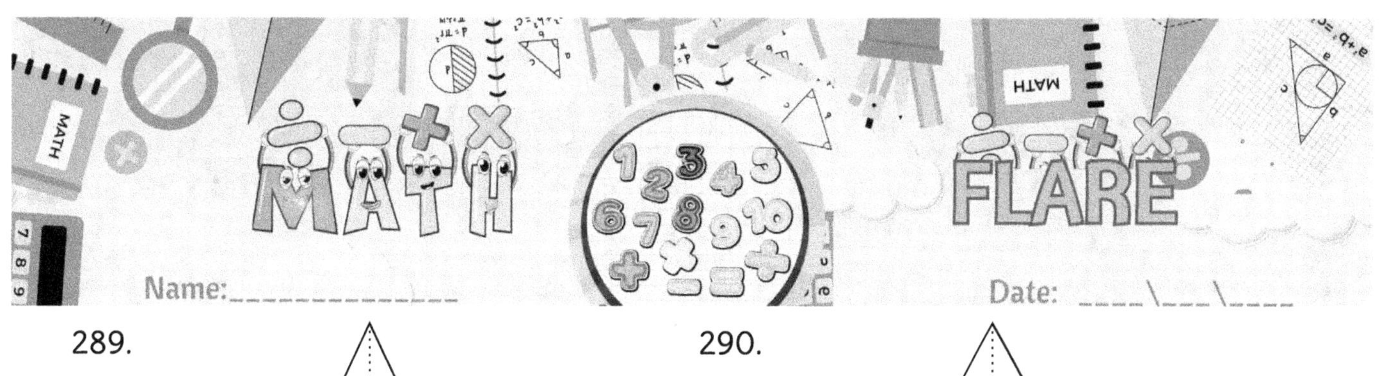

289.

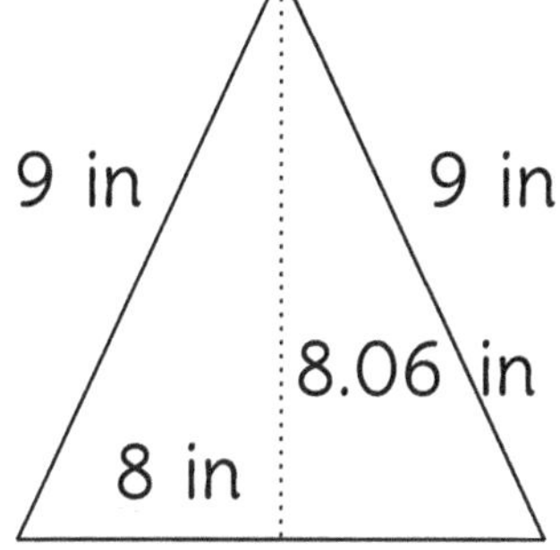

290.

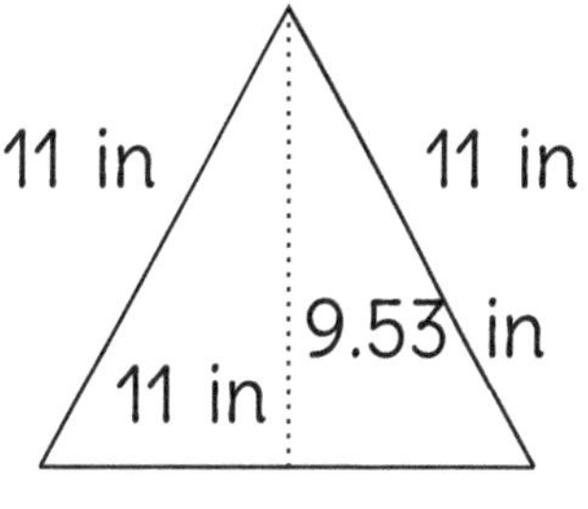

291.

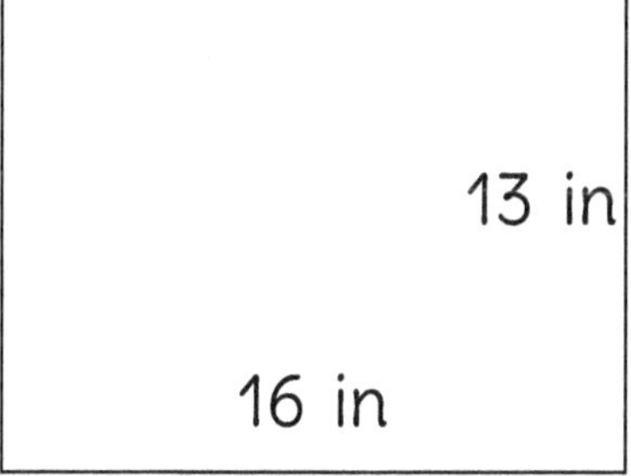

292.

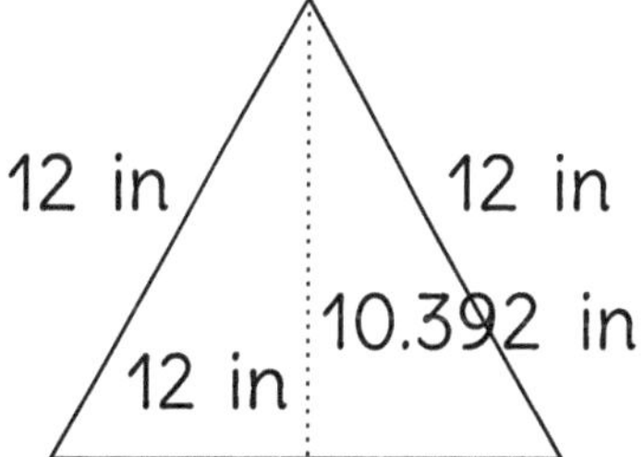

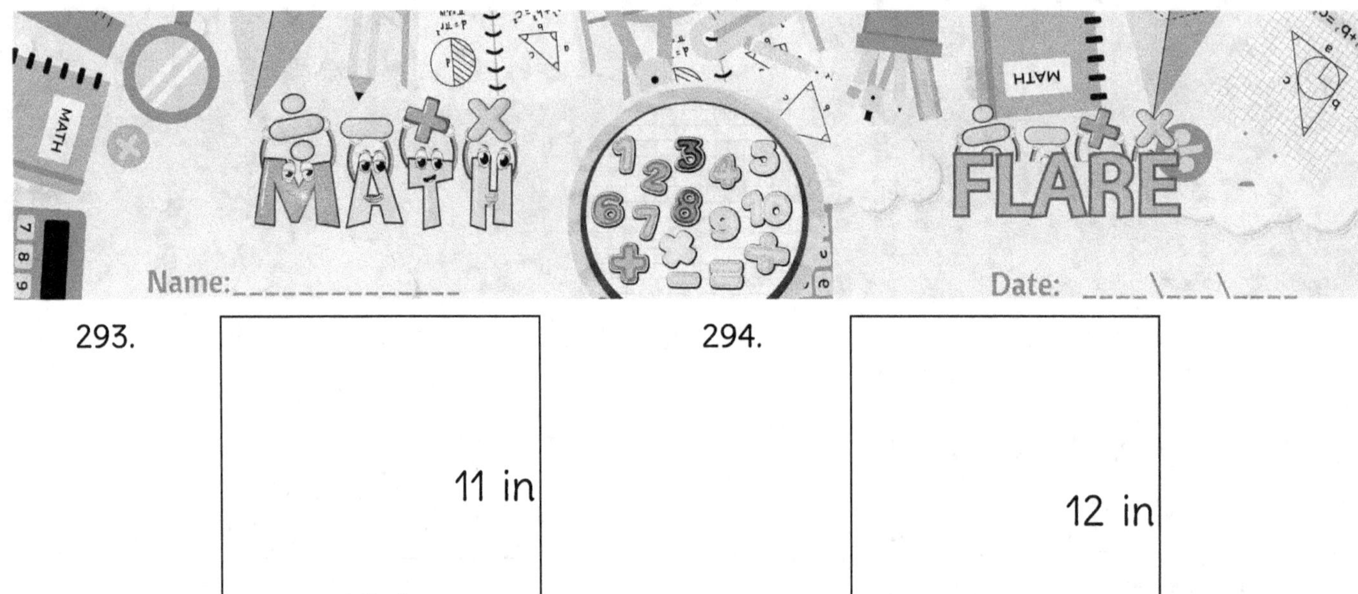

293.

11 in

10 in

294.

12 in

10 in

295.

17 in

13 in

11 in

296.

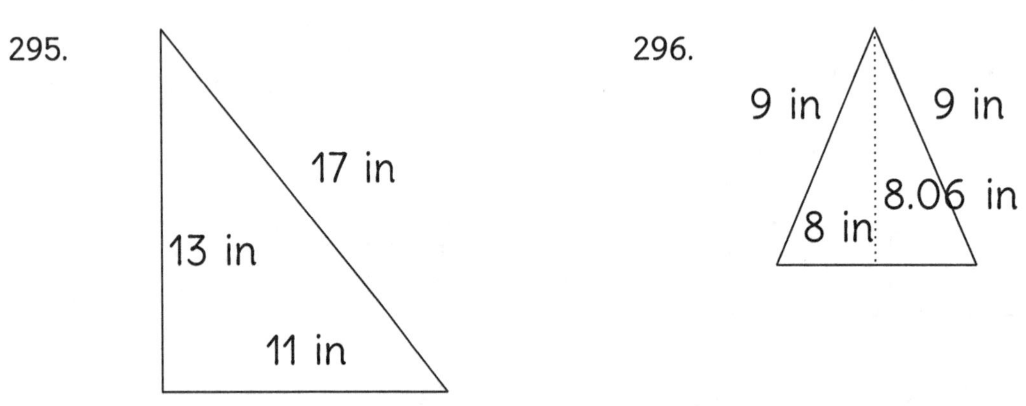

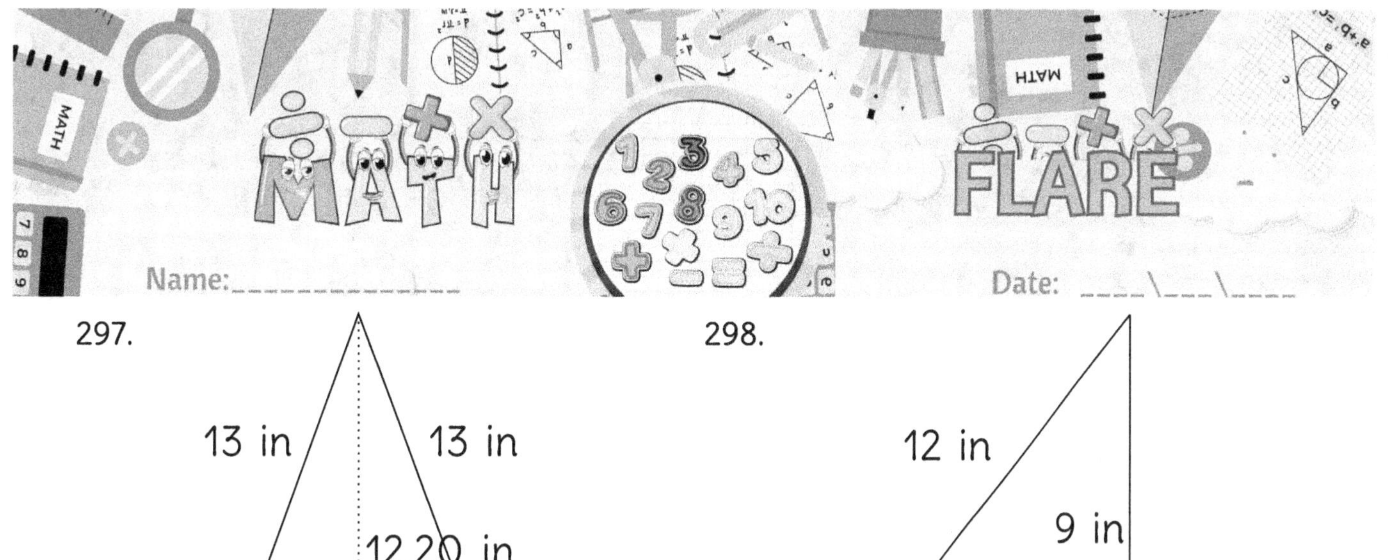

297.

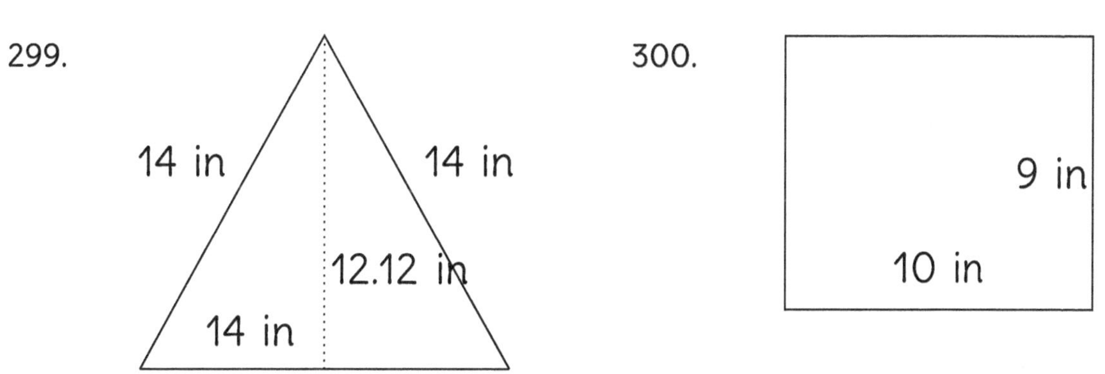

298.

299.

300.

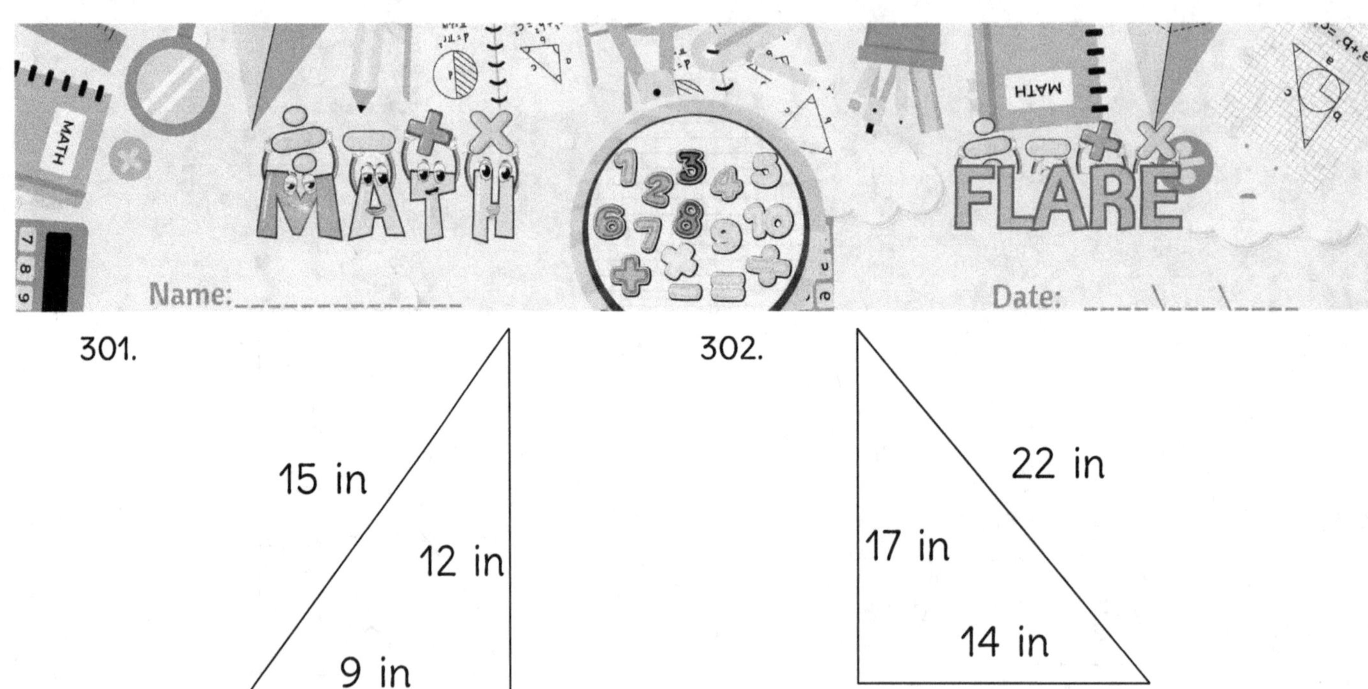

301.

302.

303.

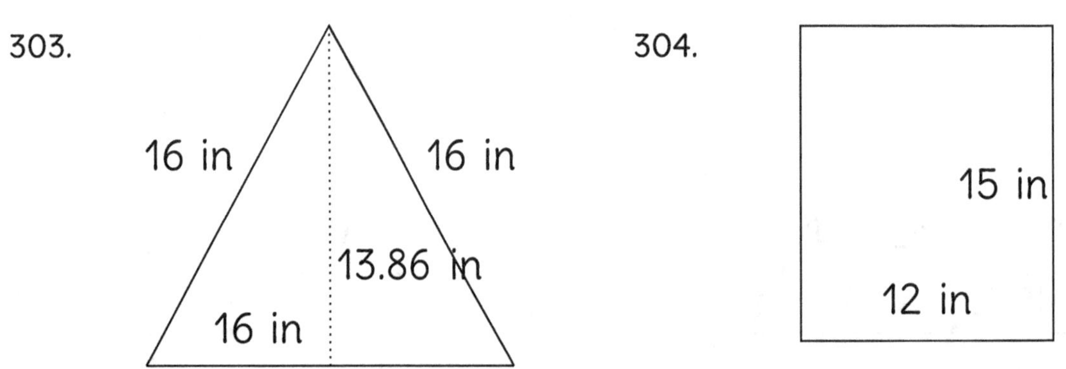

304.

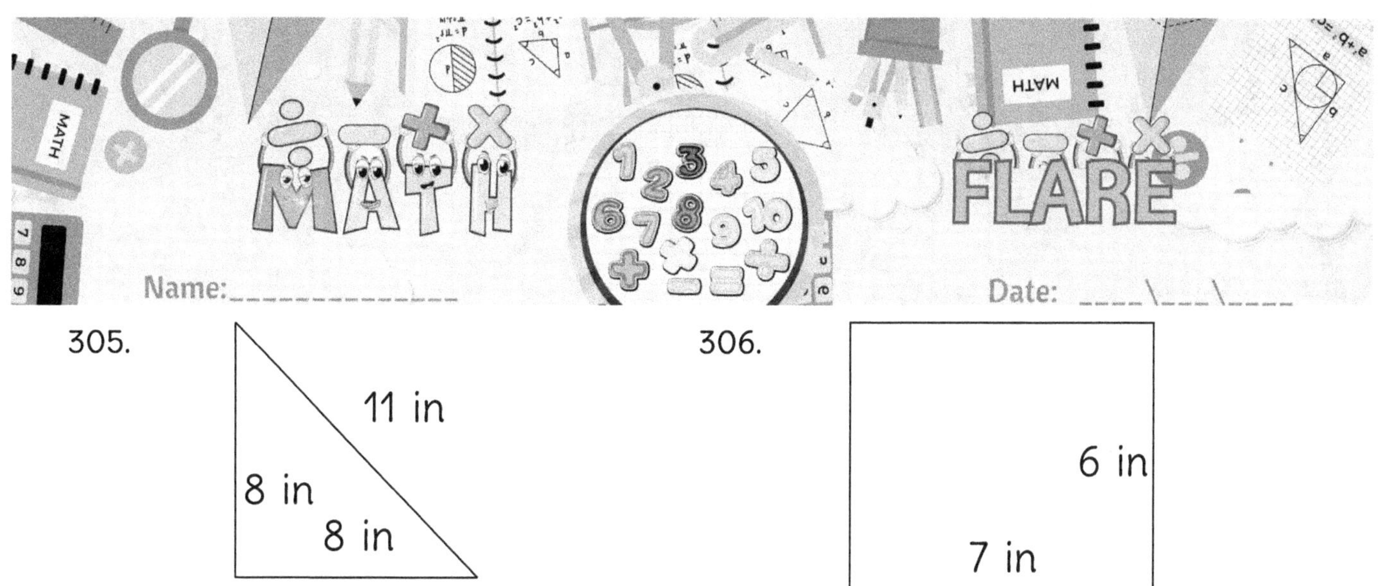

305.

306.

307.

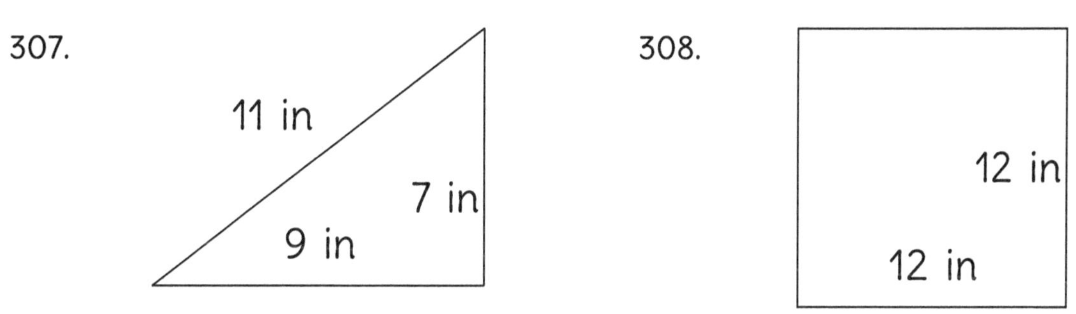

308.

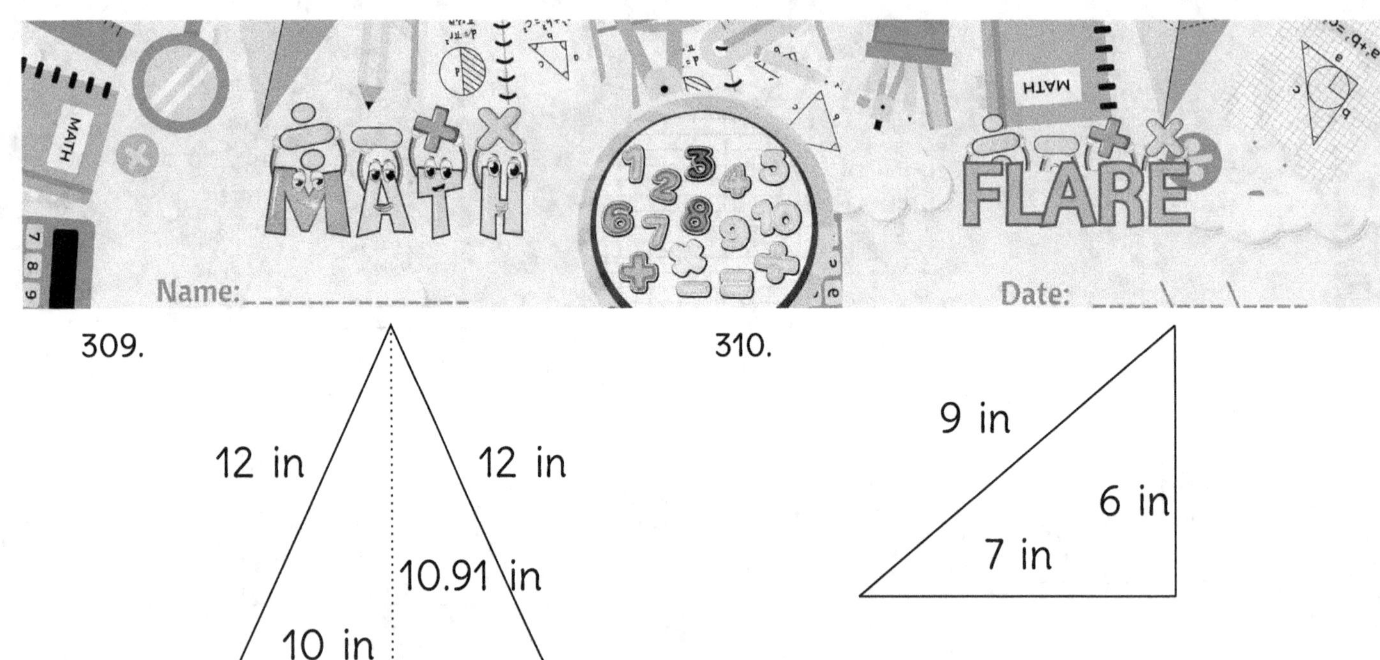

309.

310.

311.

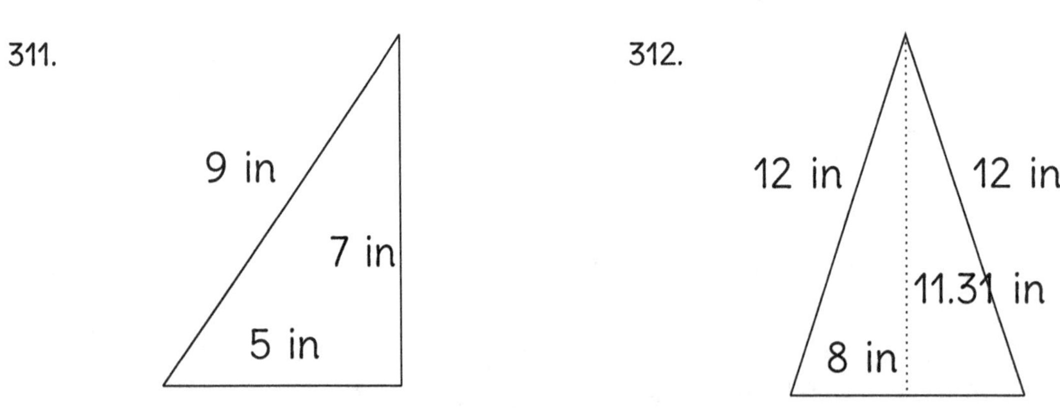

312.

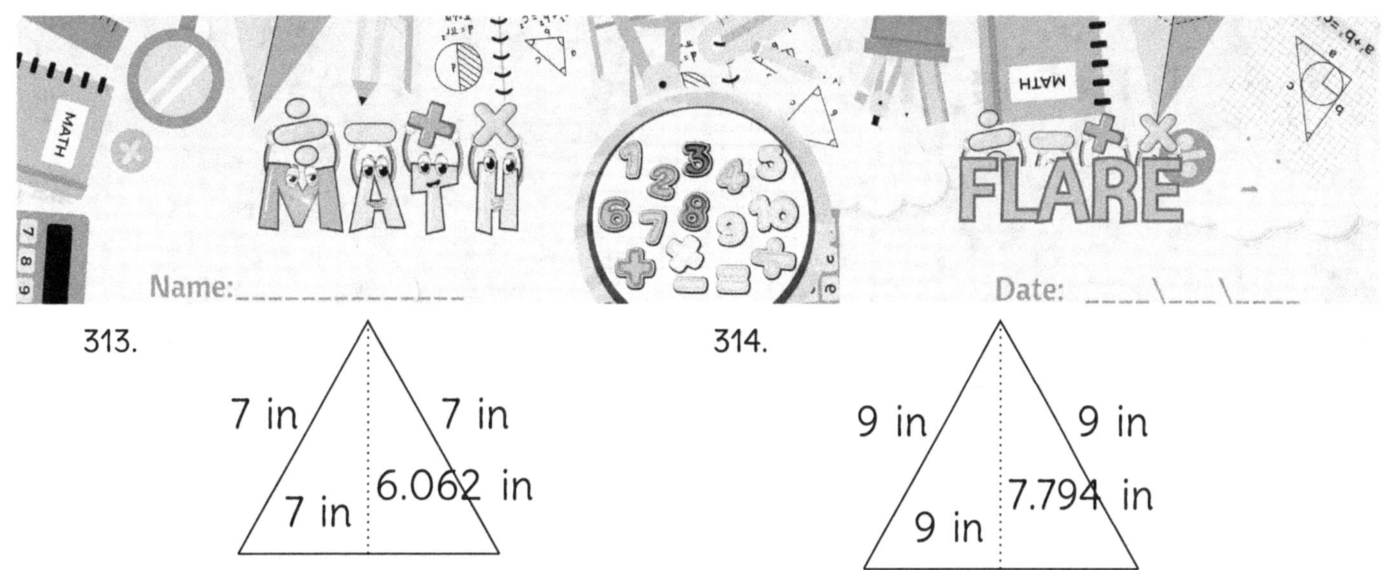

313.

7 in / 7 in
7 in | 6.062 in

314.

9 in / 9 in
9 in | 7.794 in

315.

9 in
6 in
7 in

316.

16 in / 16 in
16 in | 13.856 in

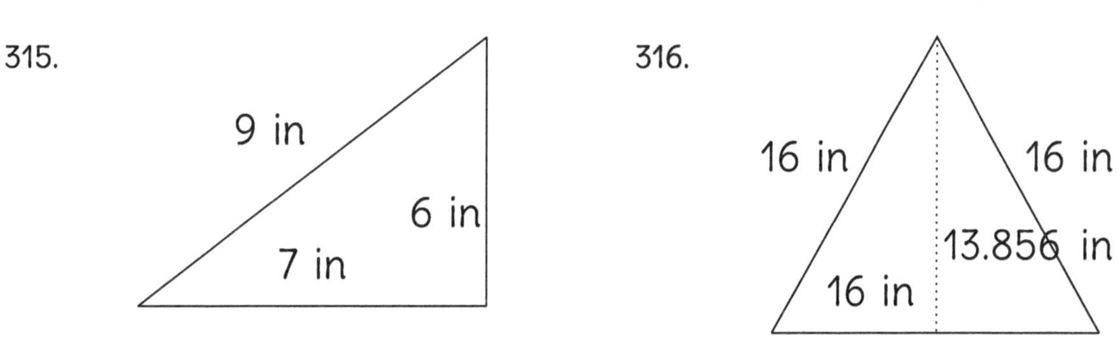

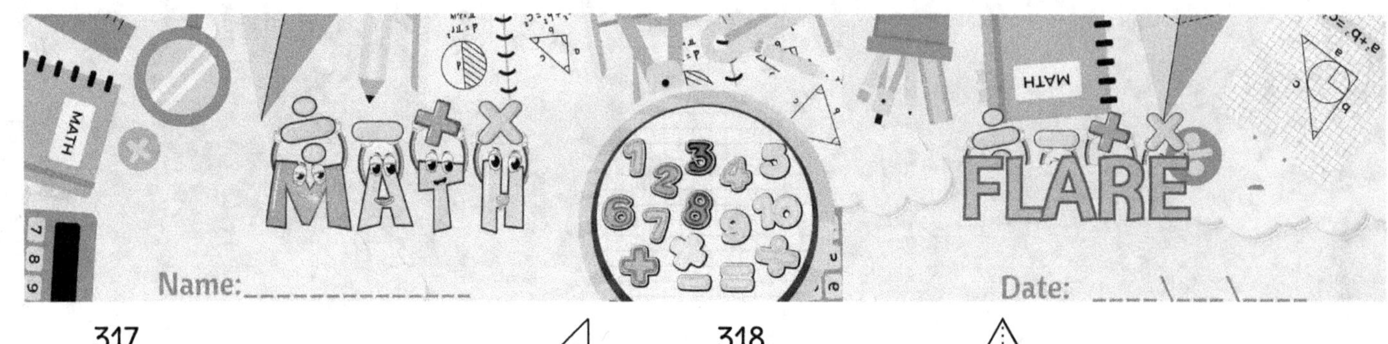

317.

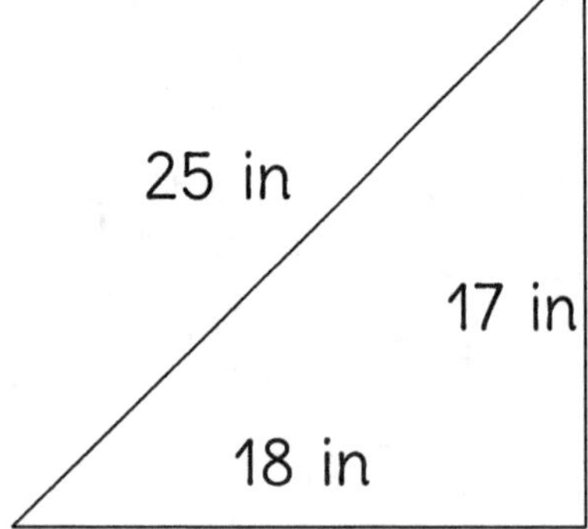

318.

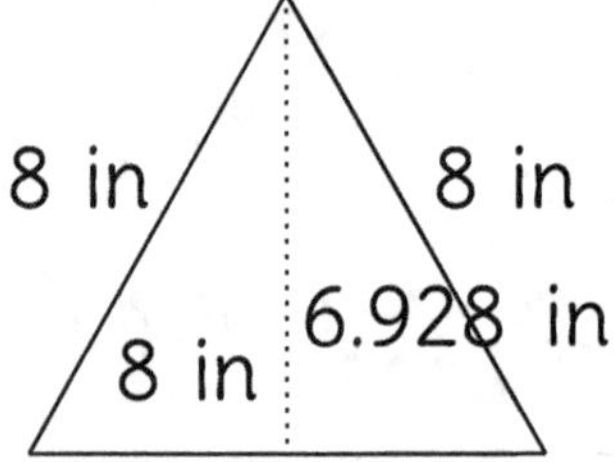

319.

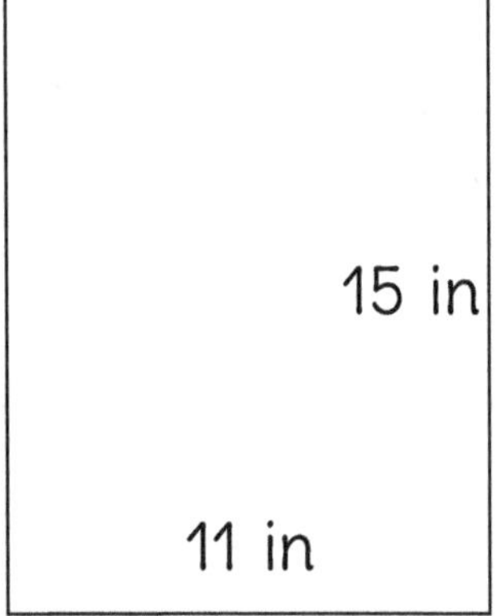

320.

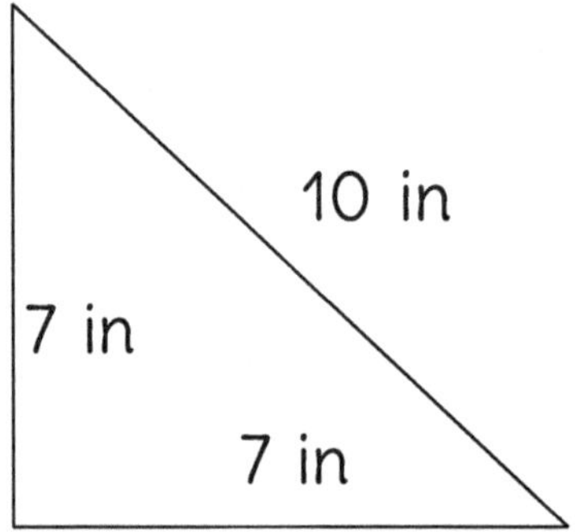

MathFlare - Units, Numerals, and Geometry

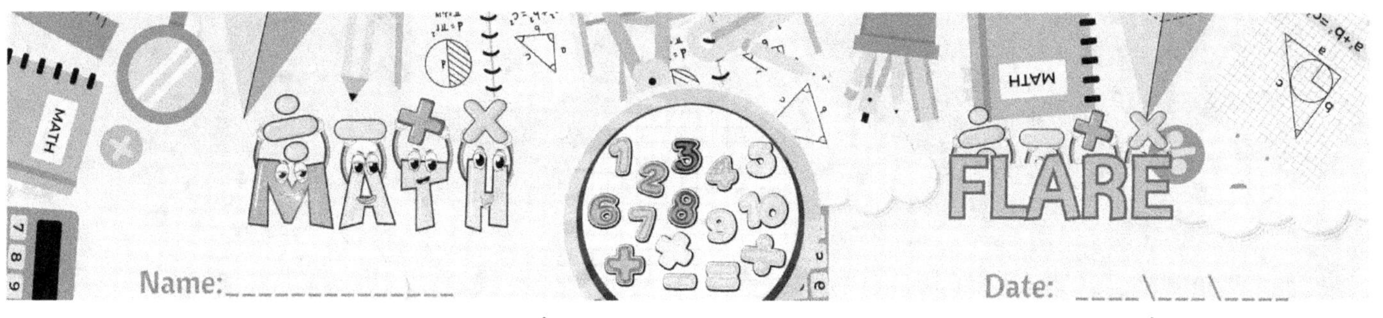

321.

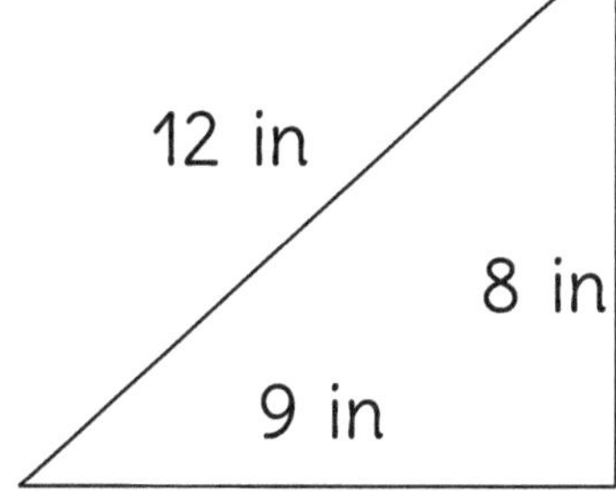

322.

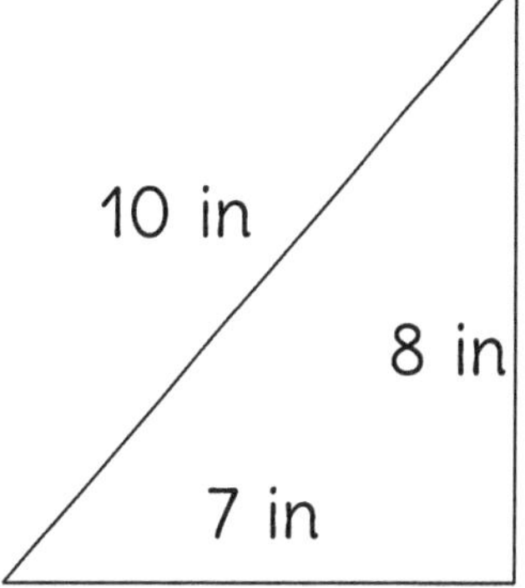

323.

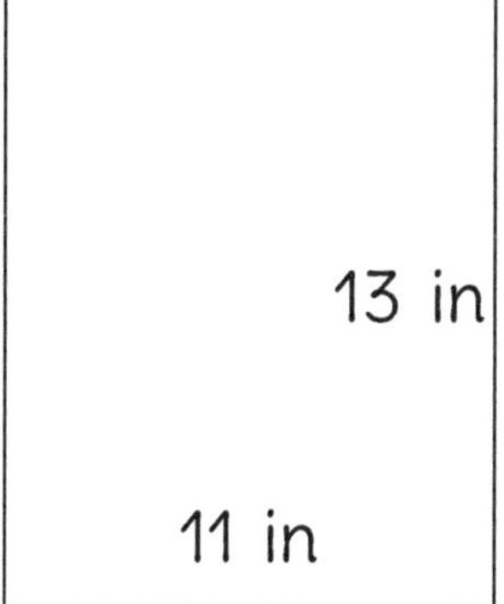

324.

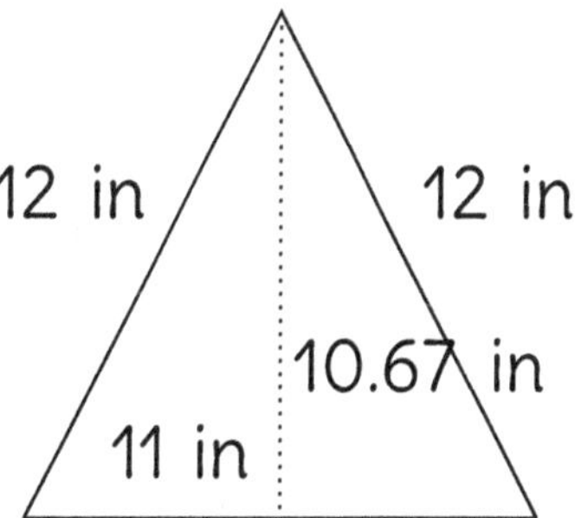

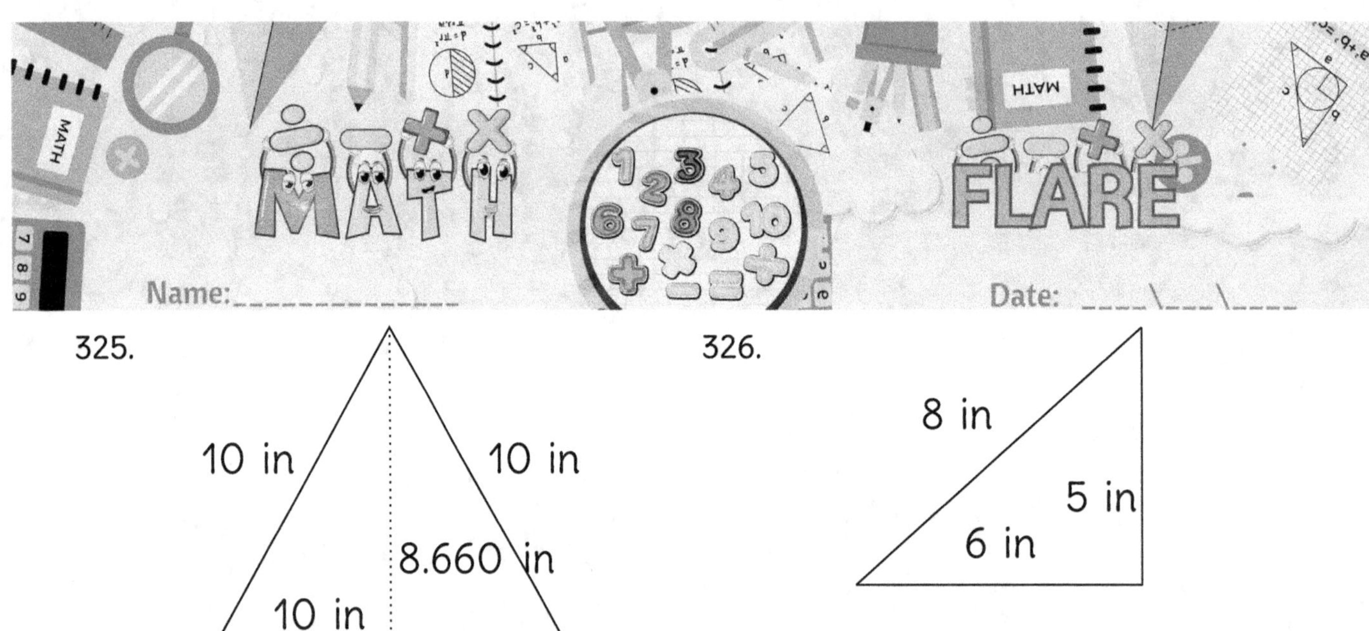

325.

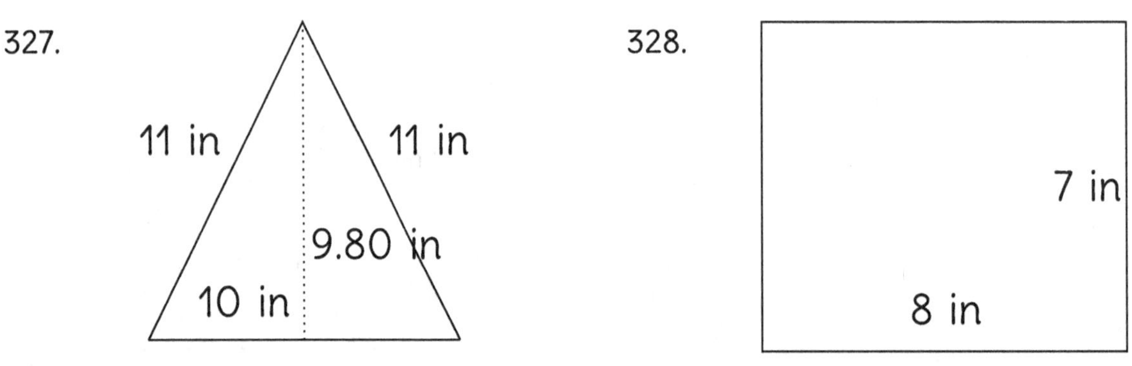

326.

327.

328.

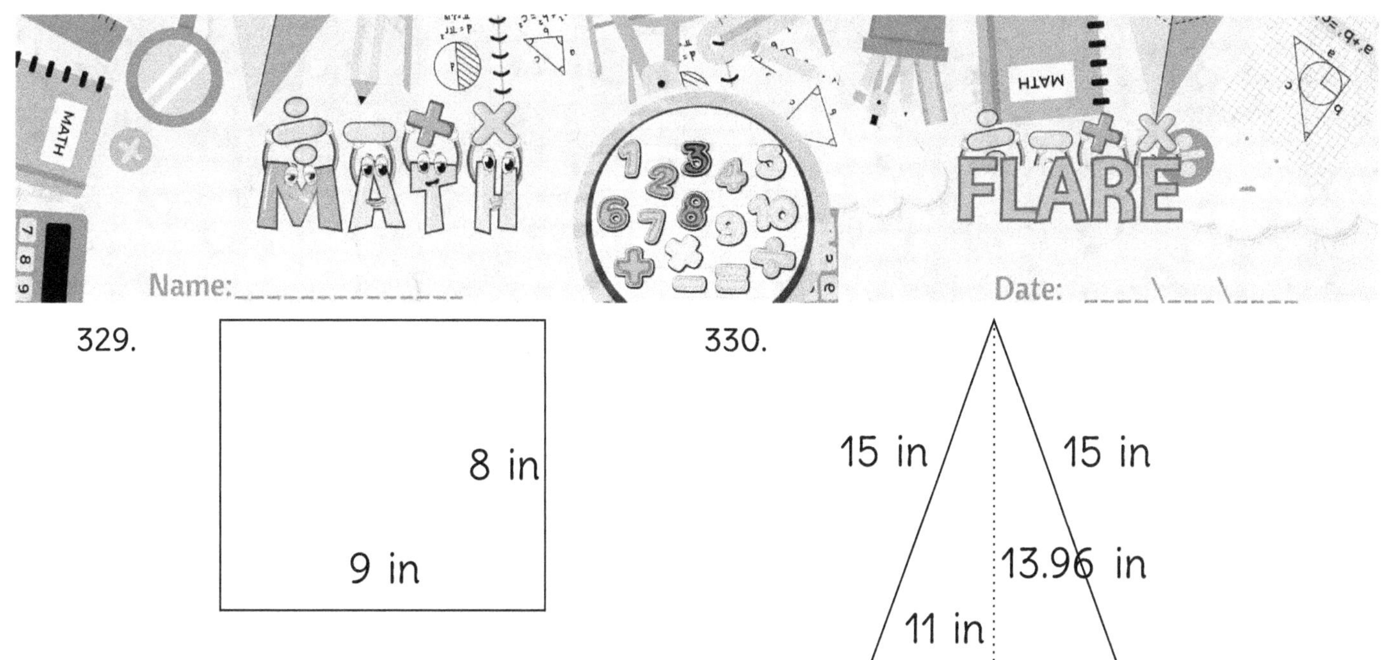

329.

8 in

9 in

330.

15 in   15 in

13.96 in

11 in

331.

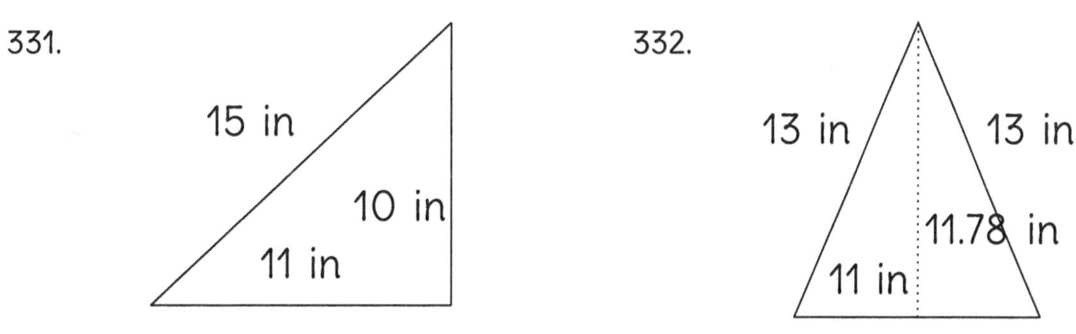

15 in

10 in

11 in

332.

13 in   13 in

11.78 in

11 in

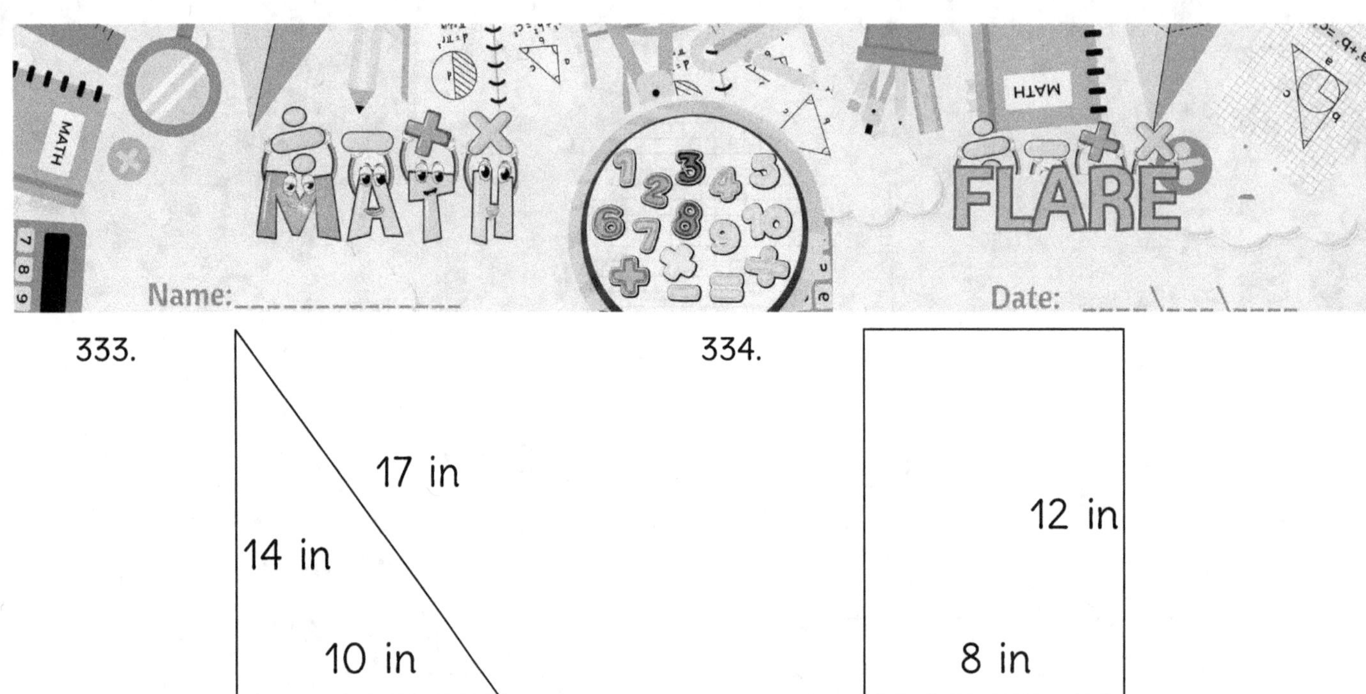

333.

17 in

14 in

10 in

334.

12 in

8 in

Volume and Surface Area

335.

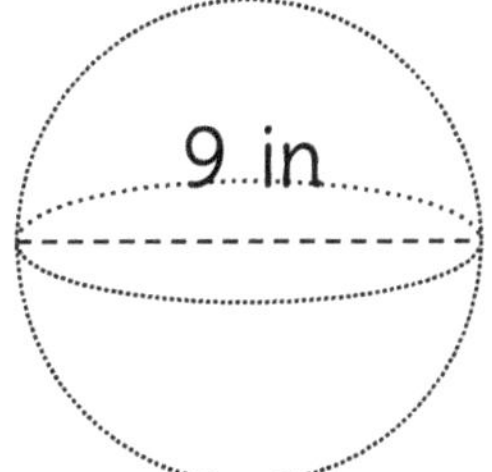

336.

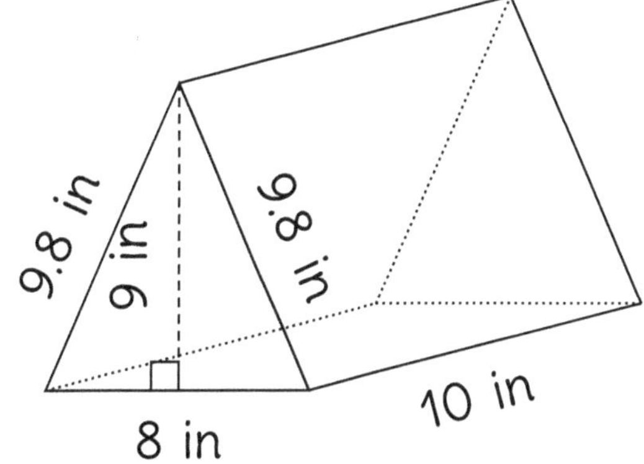

337.

338.

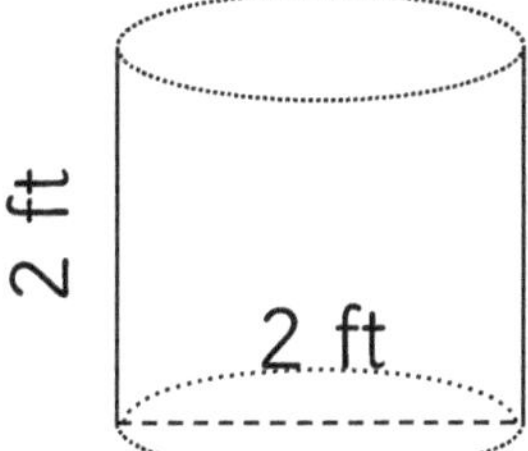

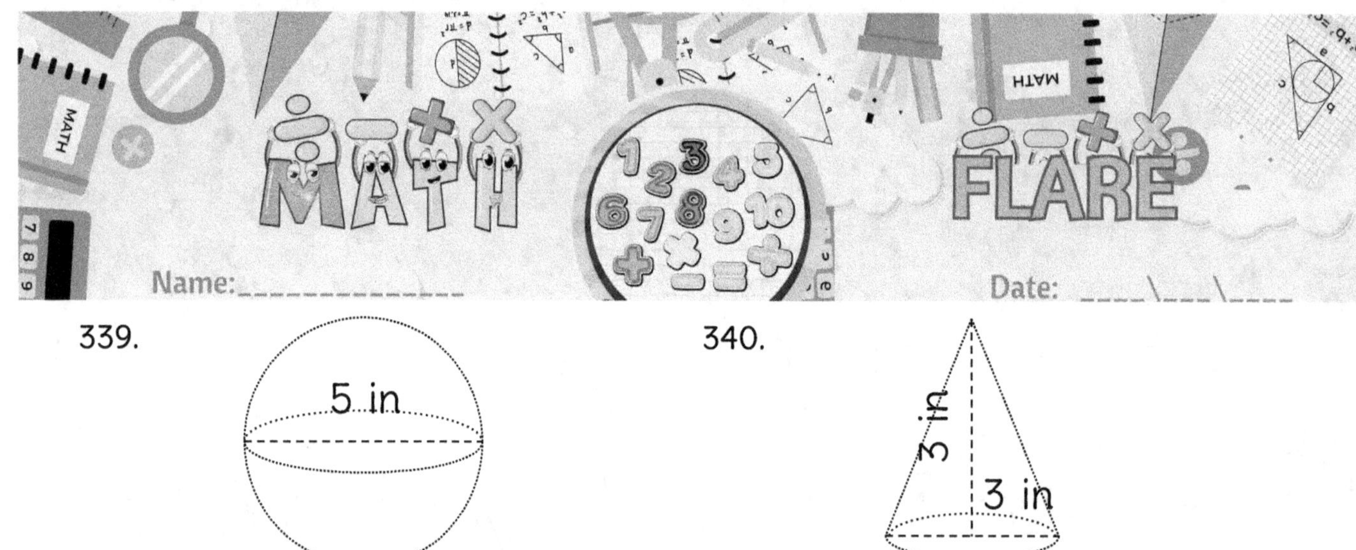

339.

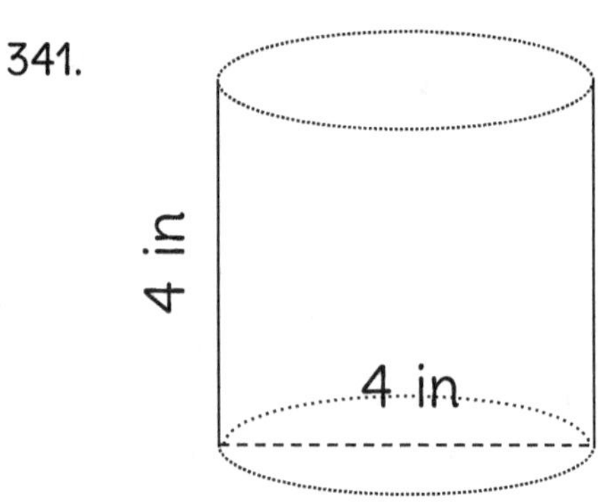

340.

341.

342.

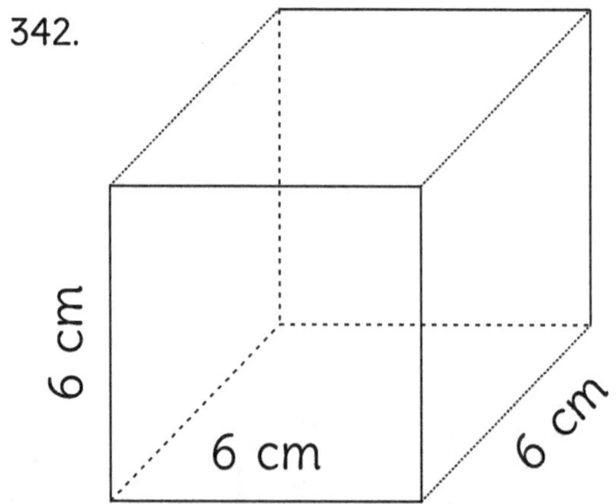

Name:
Date:
343.
4 cm
5 cm
344.
5 cm
4 cm
5 cm
6 cm
5 cm

345.

7.6 ft
7 ft
7.6 ft
6 ft
5 ft

346.

5 in
4 in
4 in

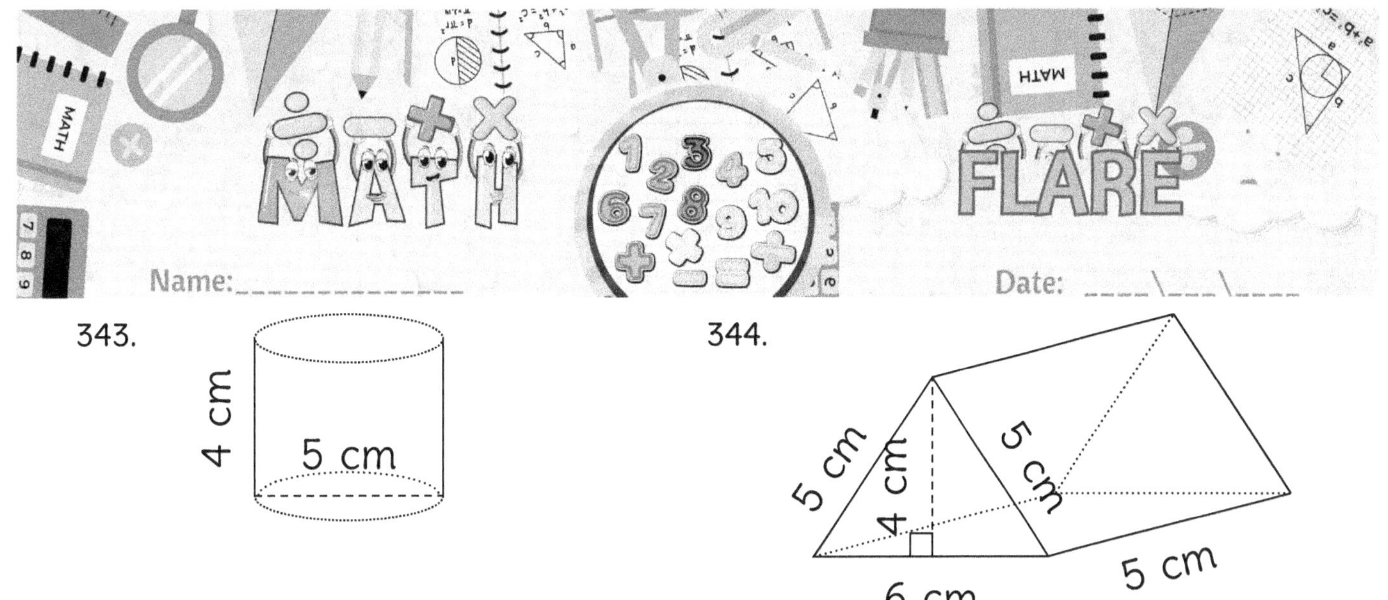

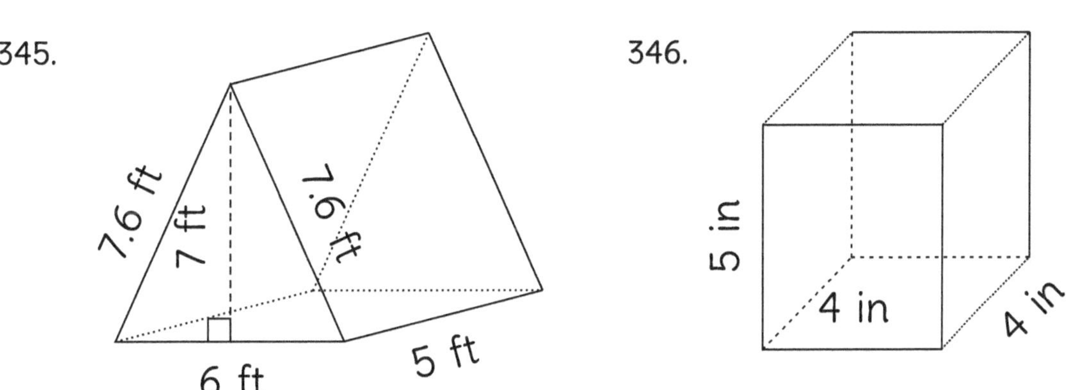

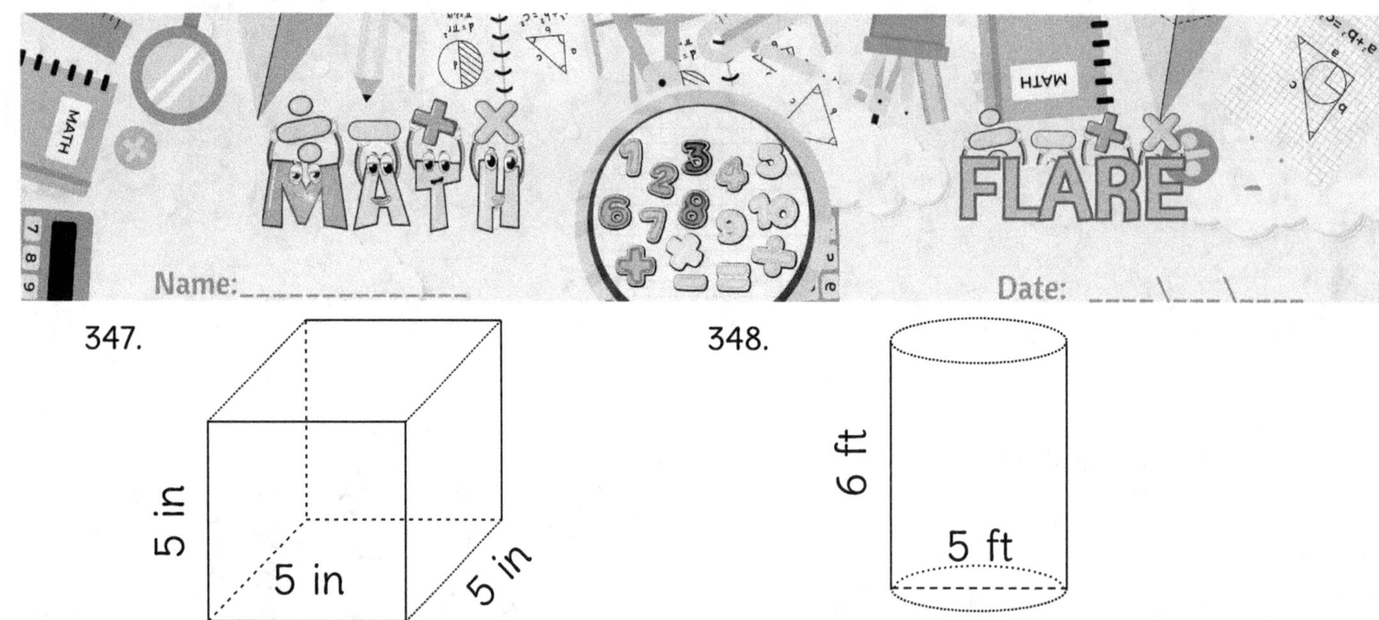

347.

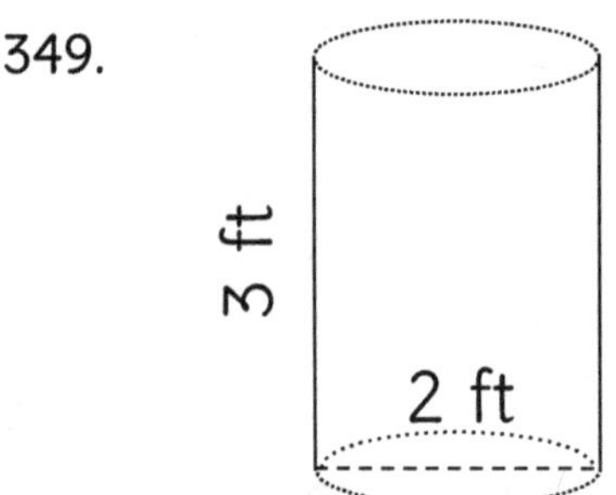

348.

349.

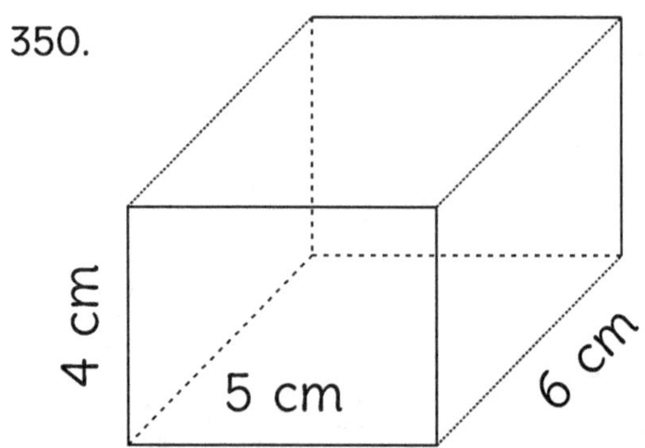

350.

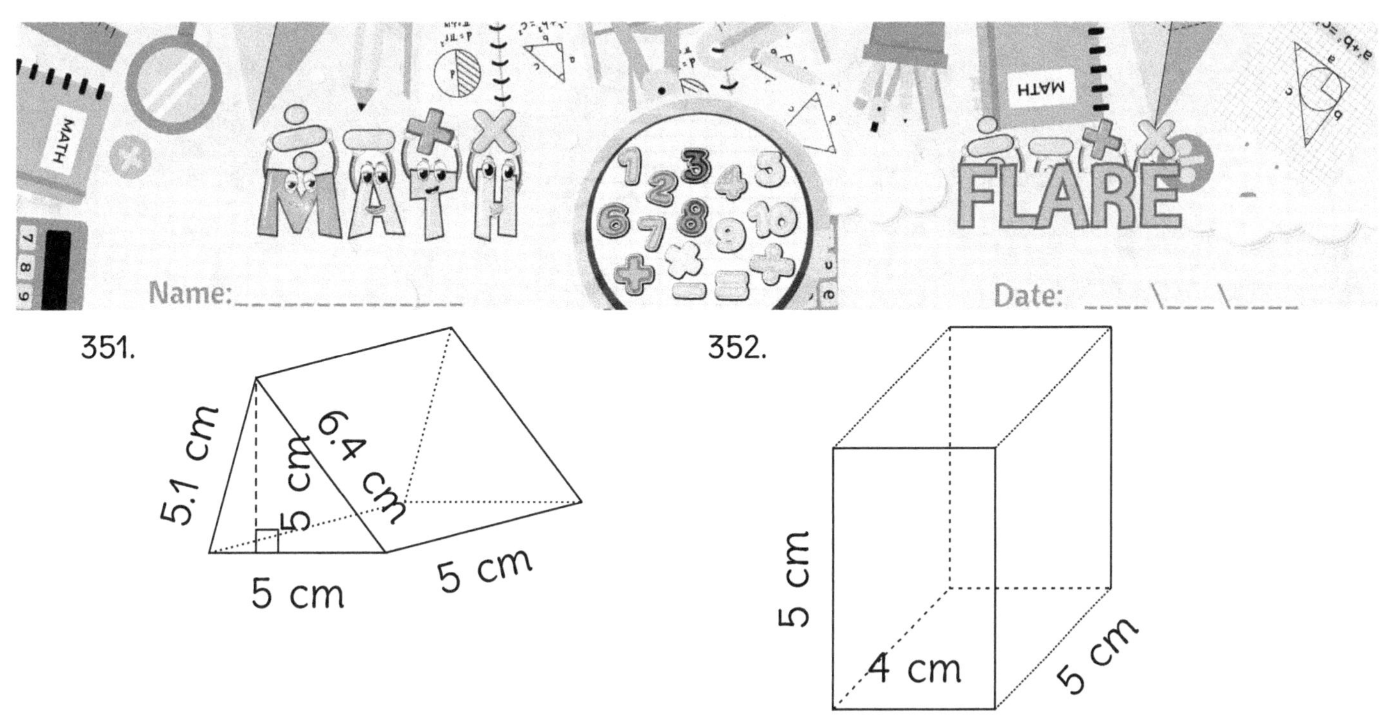

351.

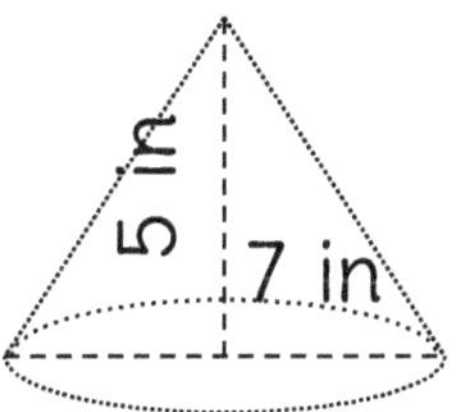

352.

353.

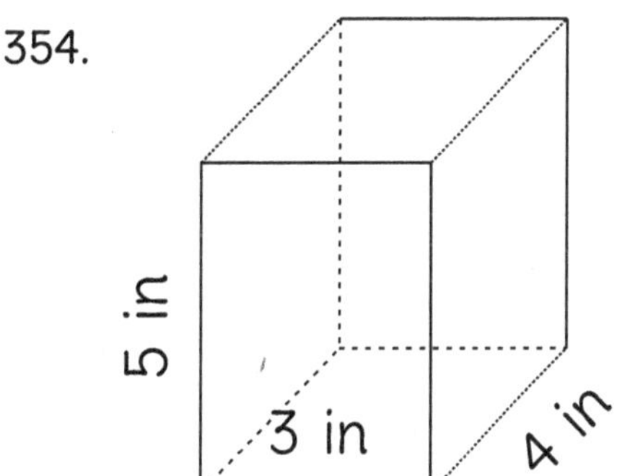

354.

355.

6.3 ft
6.3 ft
6 ft
4 ft
6 ft
356.
6 cm
7 cm
6 cm

357.

2 in
2 in
3 in
358.
3 ft
5 ft
5 ft

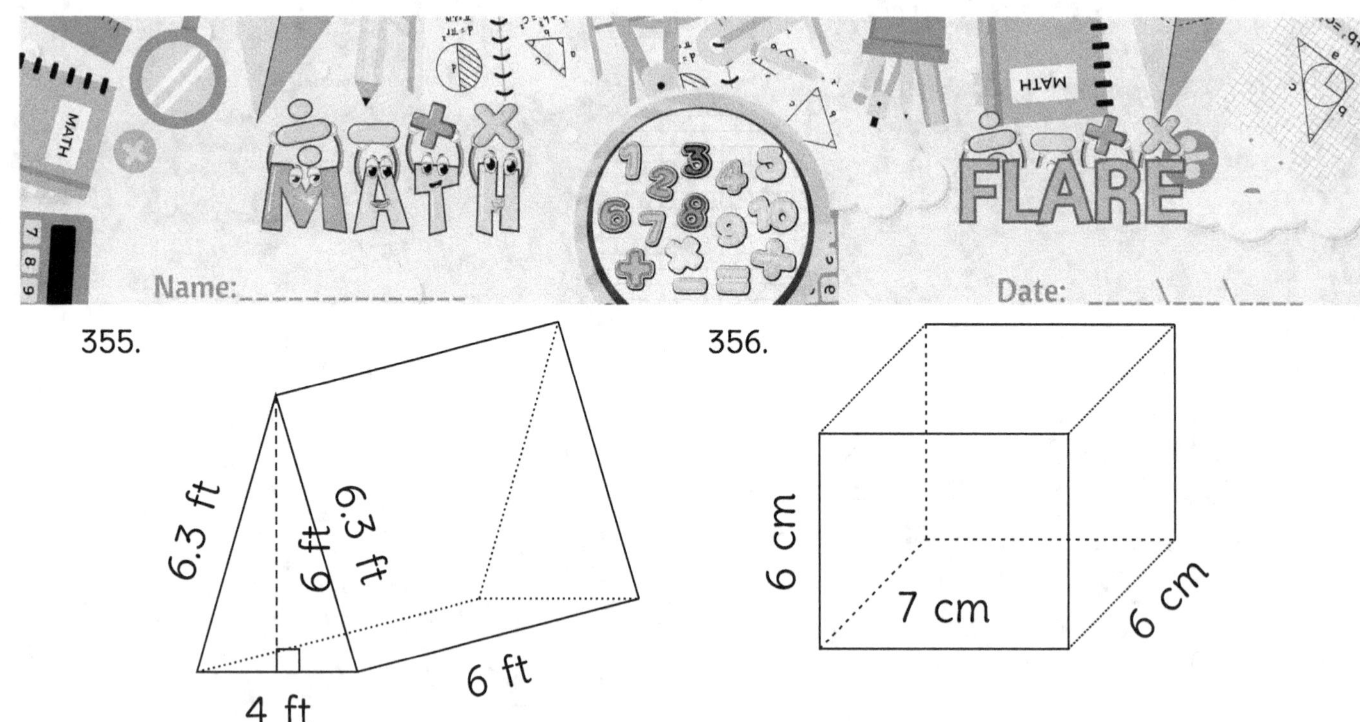

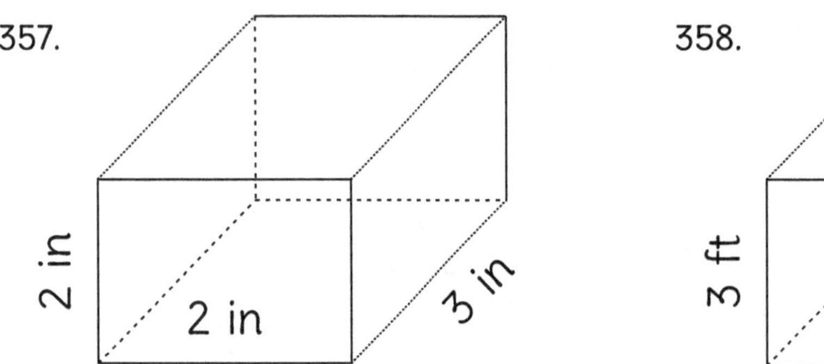

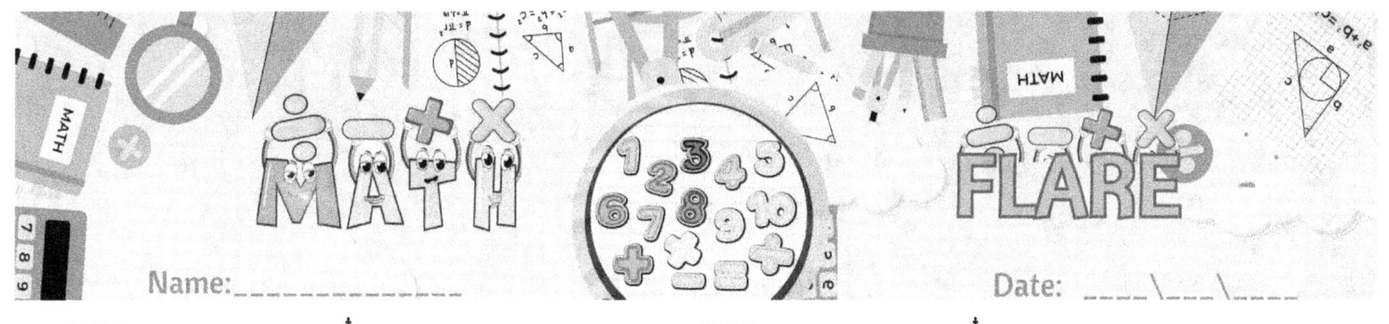

359.

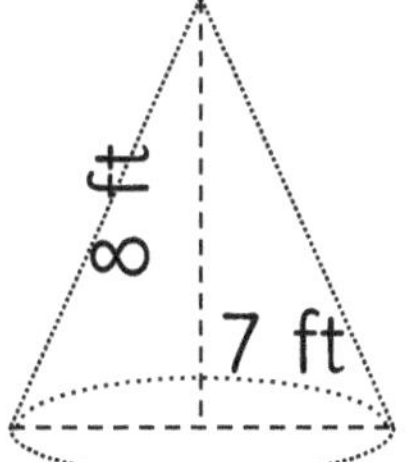

360.

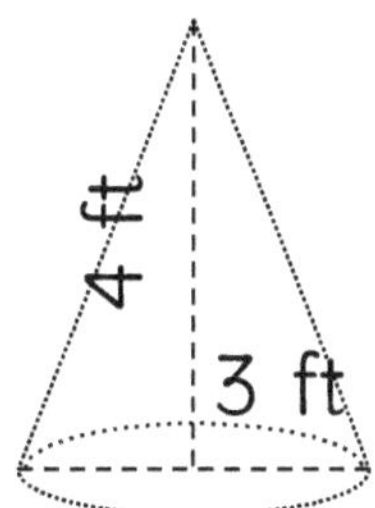

361.

362.

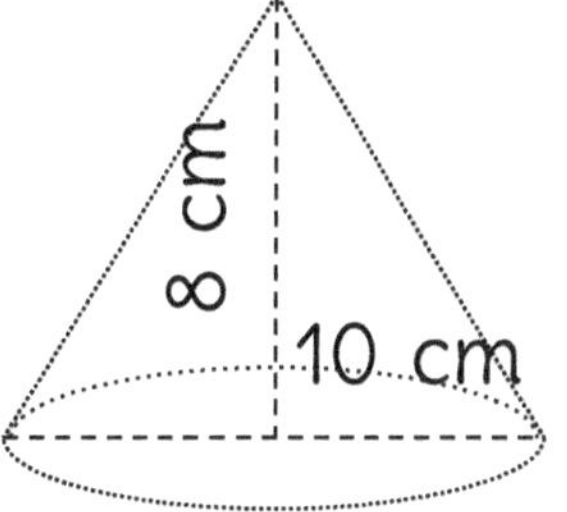

363.

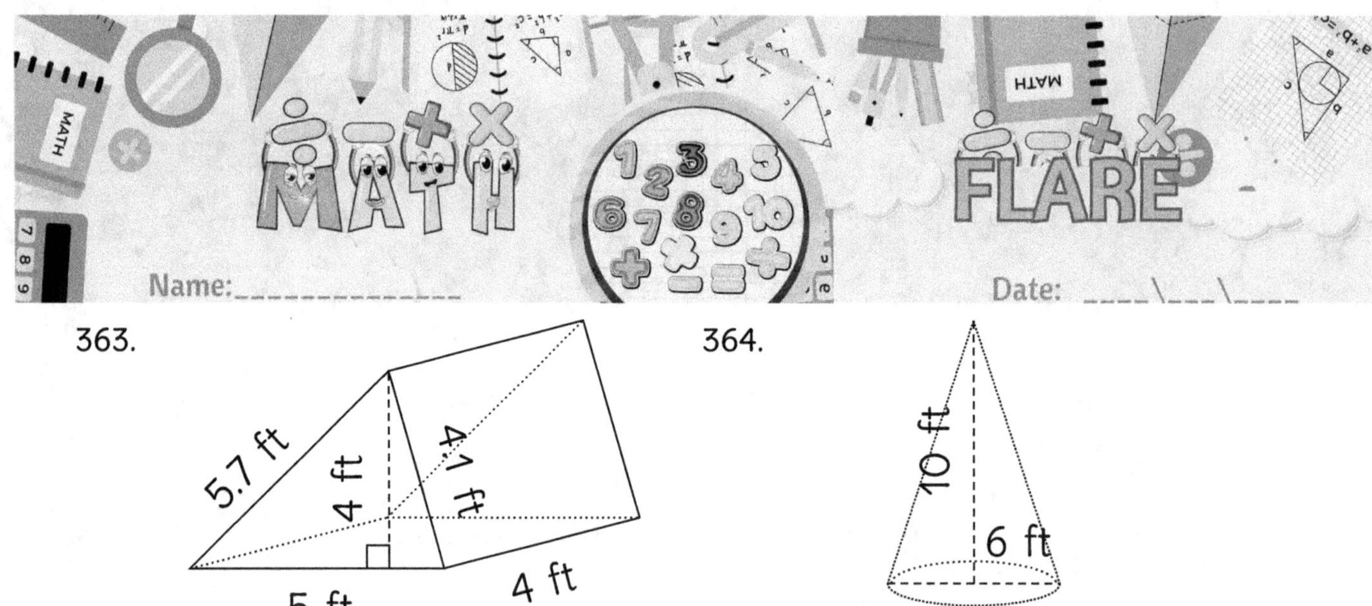

364.

365.

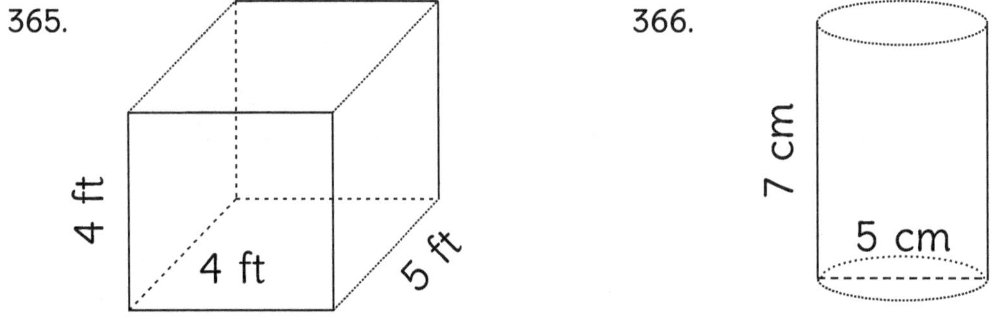

366.

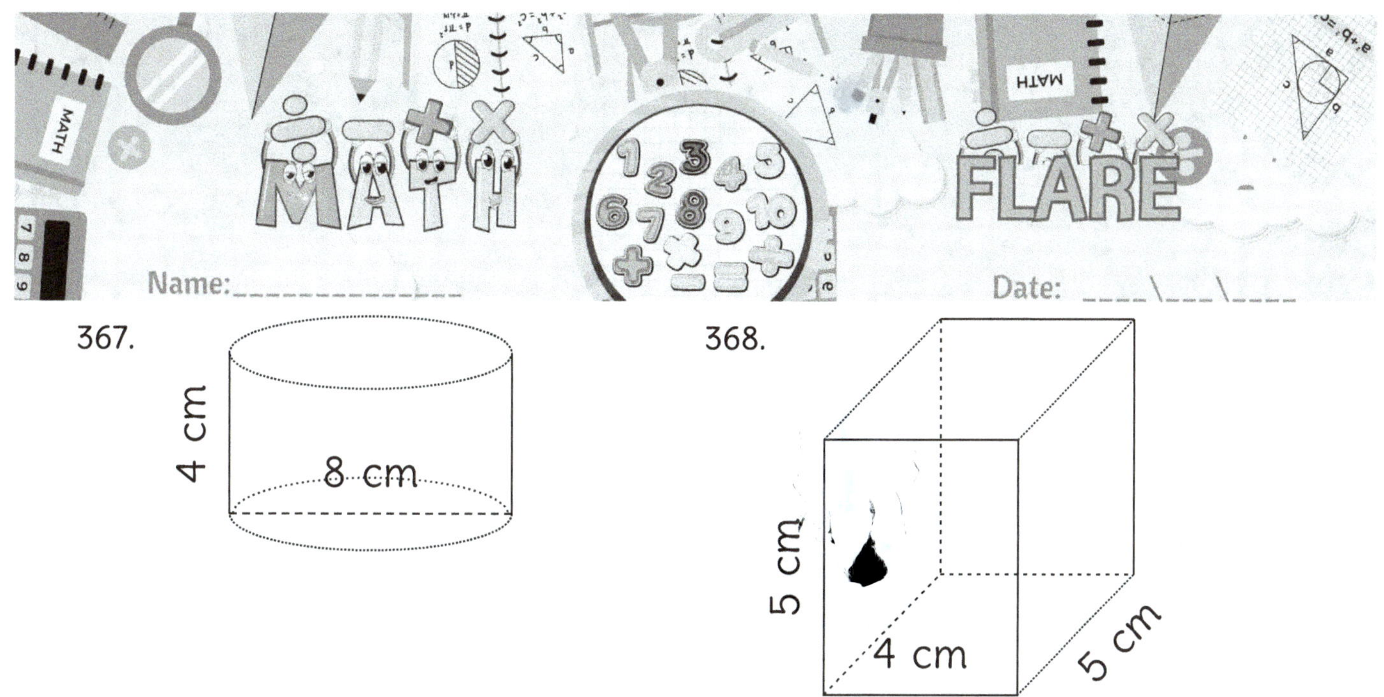

367.

368.

369.

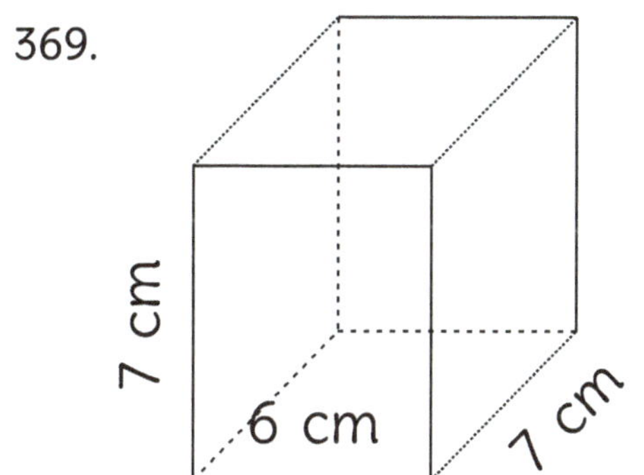

370.

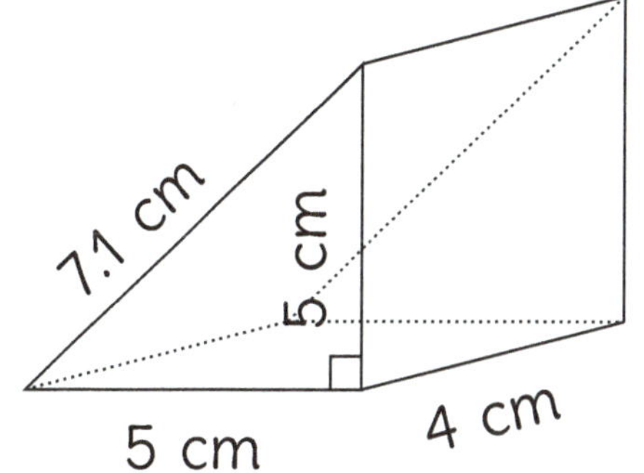

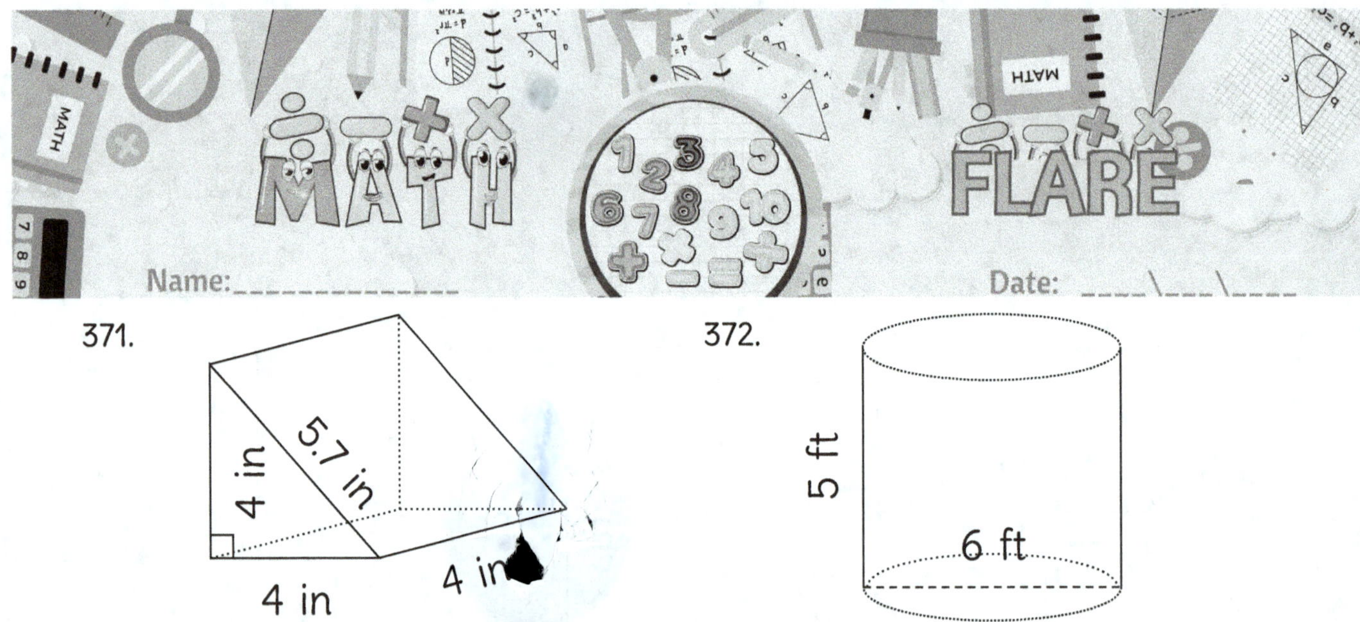

371.

372.

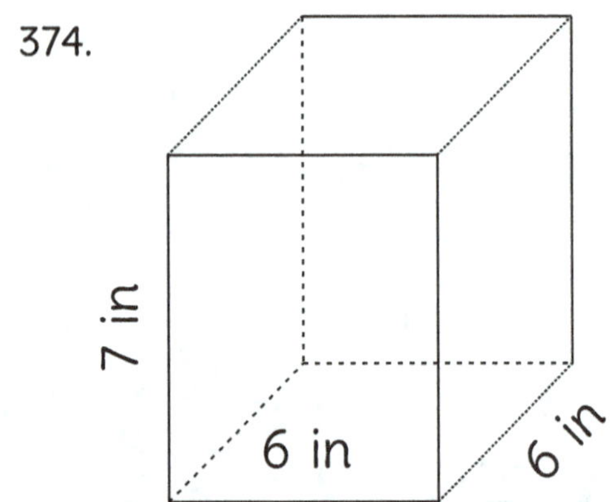

373.

374.

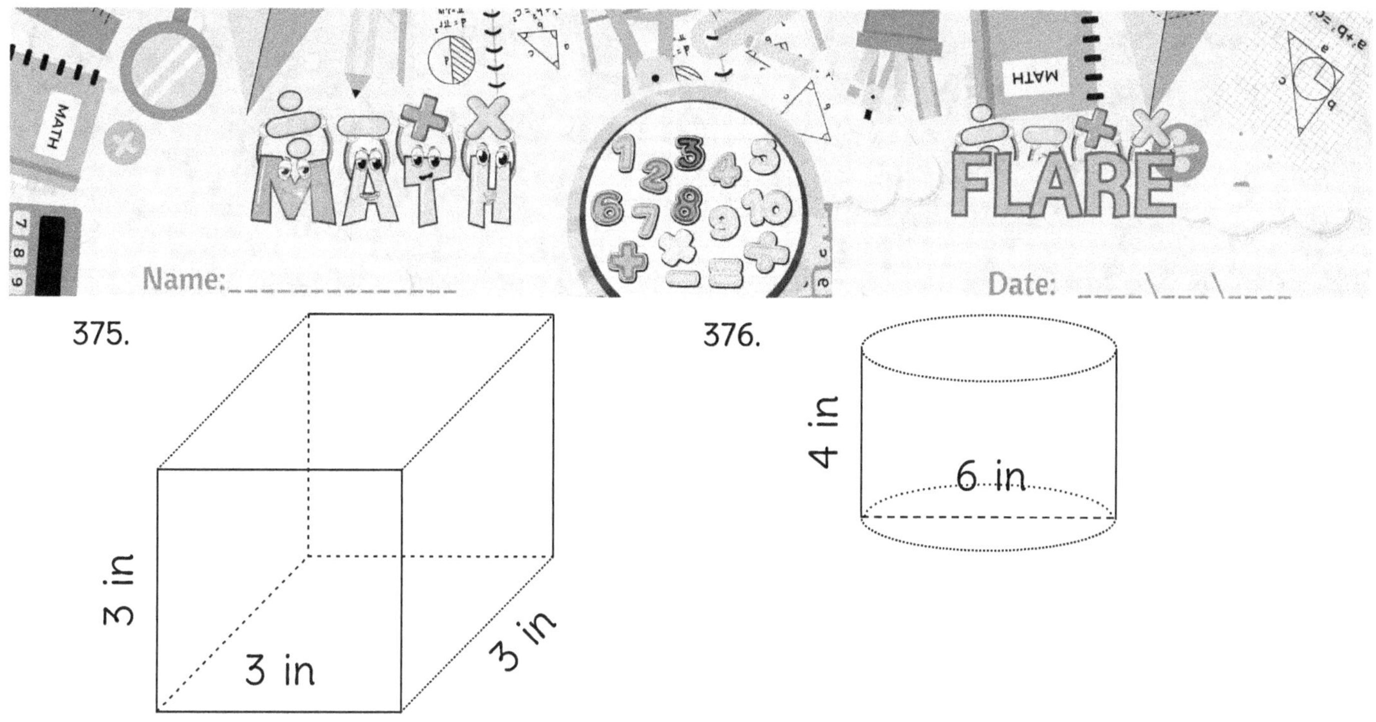

375.

3 in
3 in
3 in

376.

4 in
6 in

377.

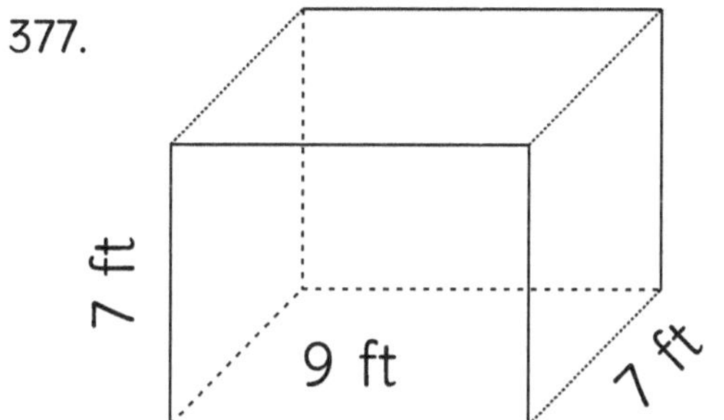

378.

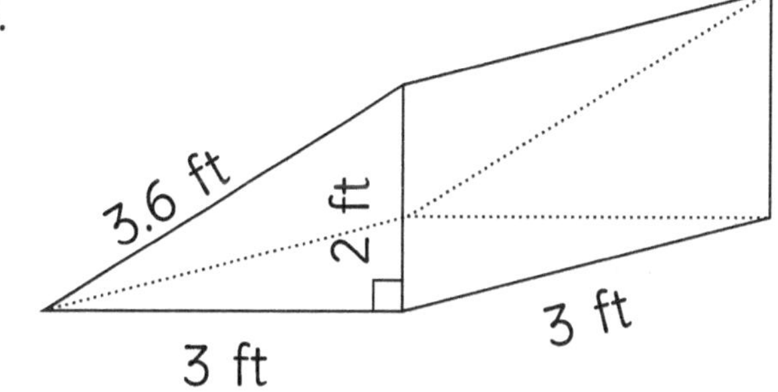

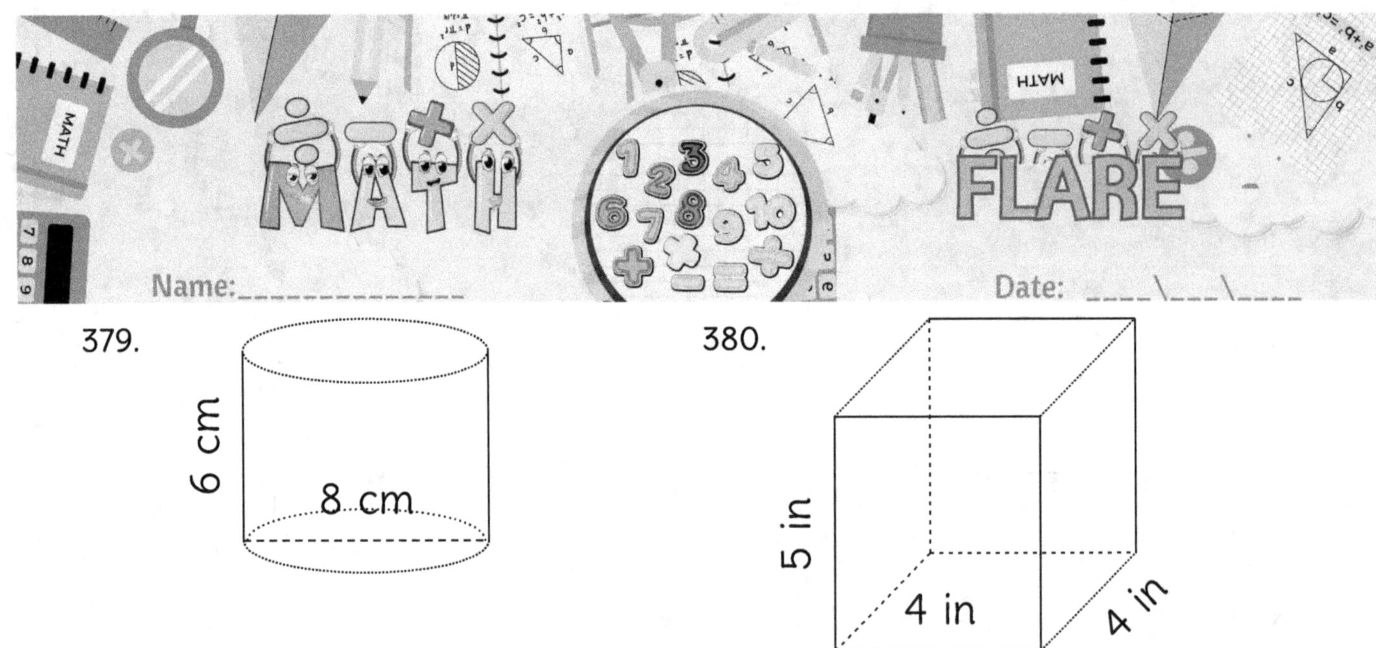

379.

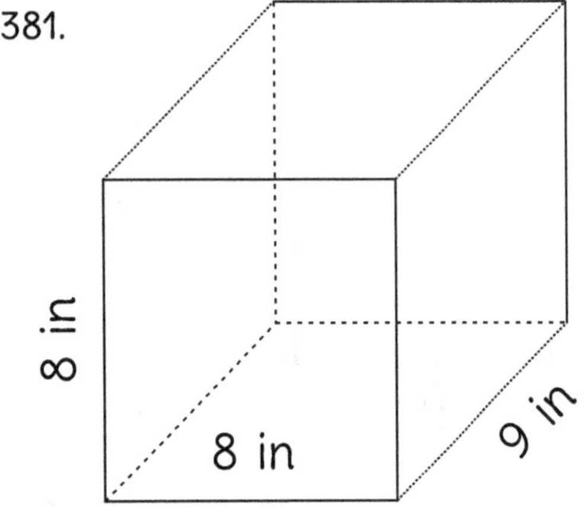

380.

381.

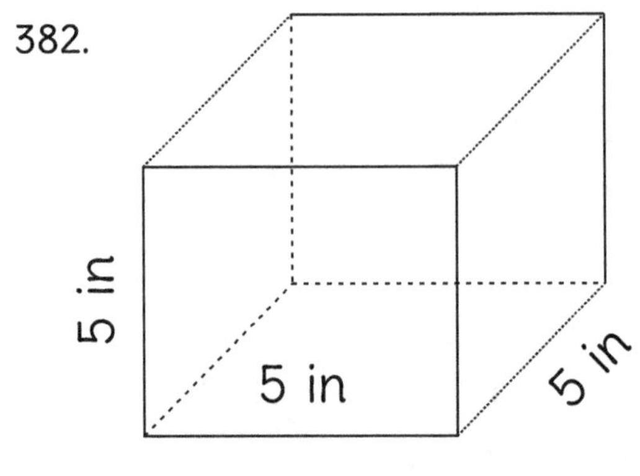

382.

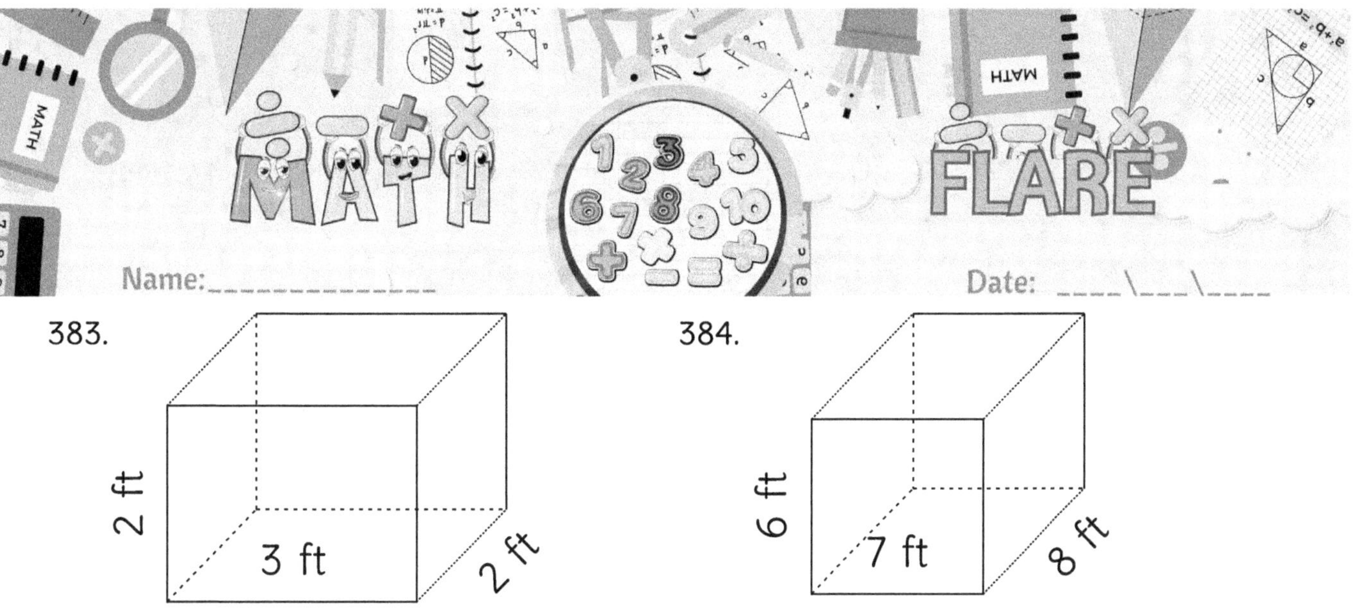

383.

384.

385.
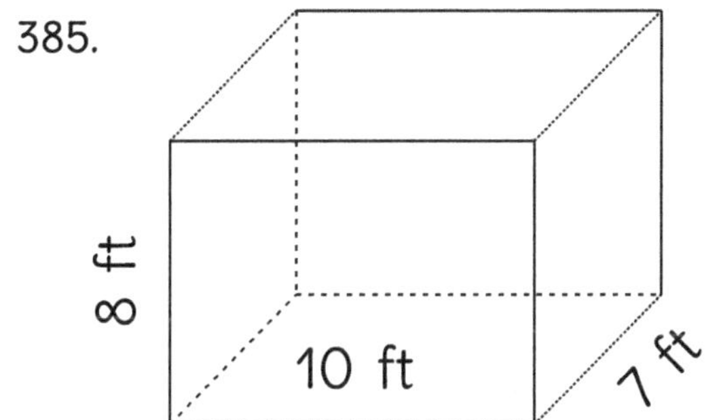

386.
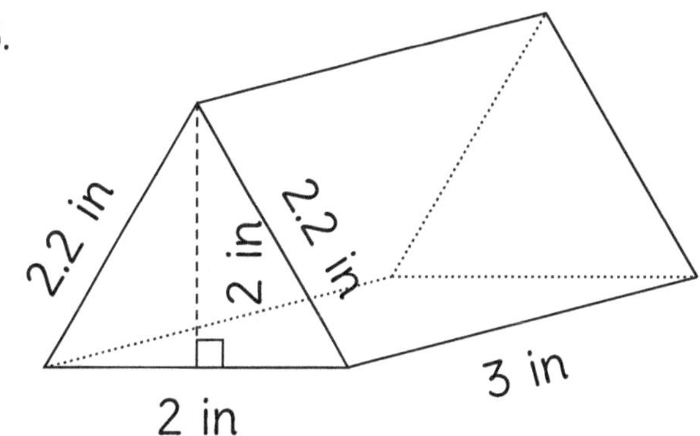

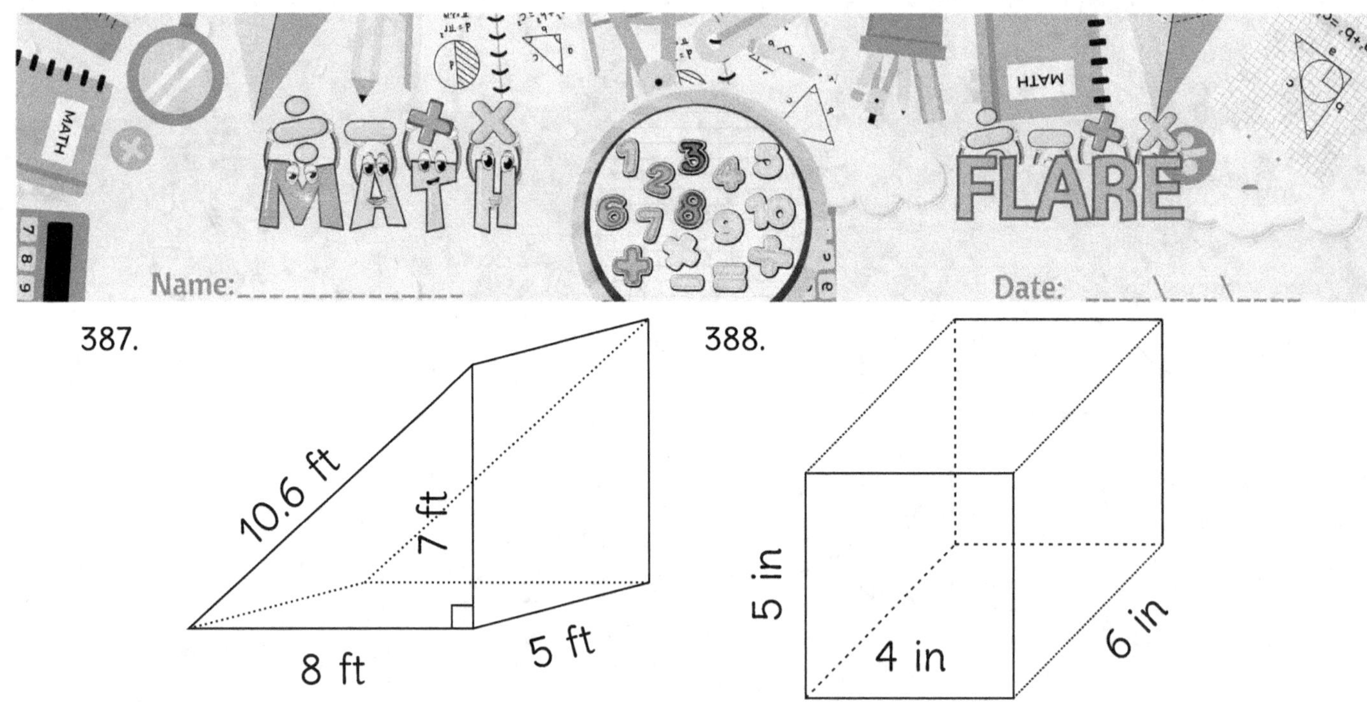

387.

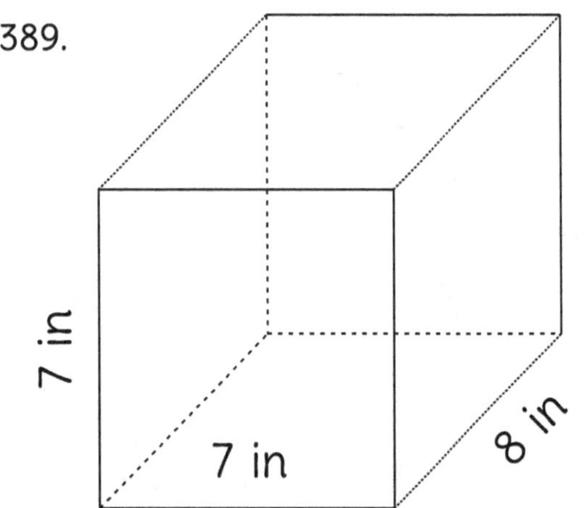

388.

389.

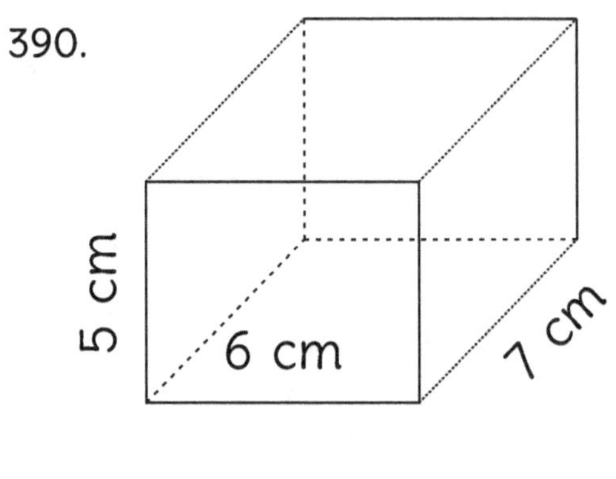

390.

Name:
Date:
391.
11.4 cm
9 cm
9.5 cm
10 cm
9 cm
392.
5.4 cm
5 cm
8.6 cm
9 cm
9 cm

393.

10 cm
10 cm
394.
3 in
4 in
5 in

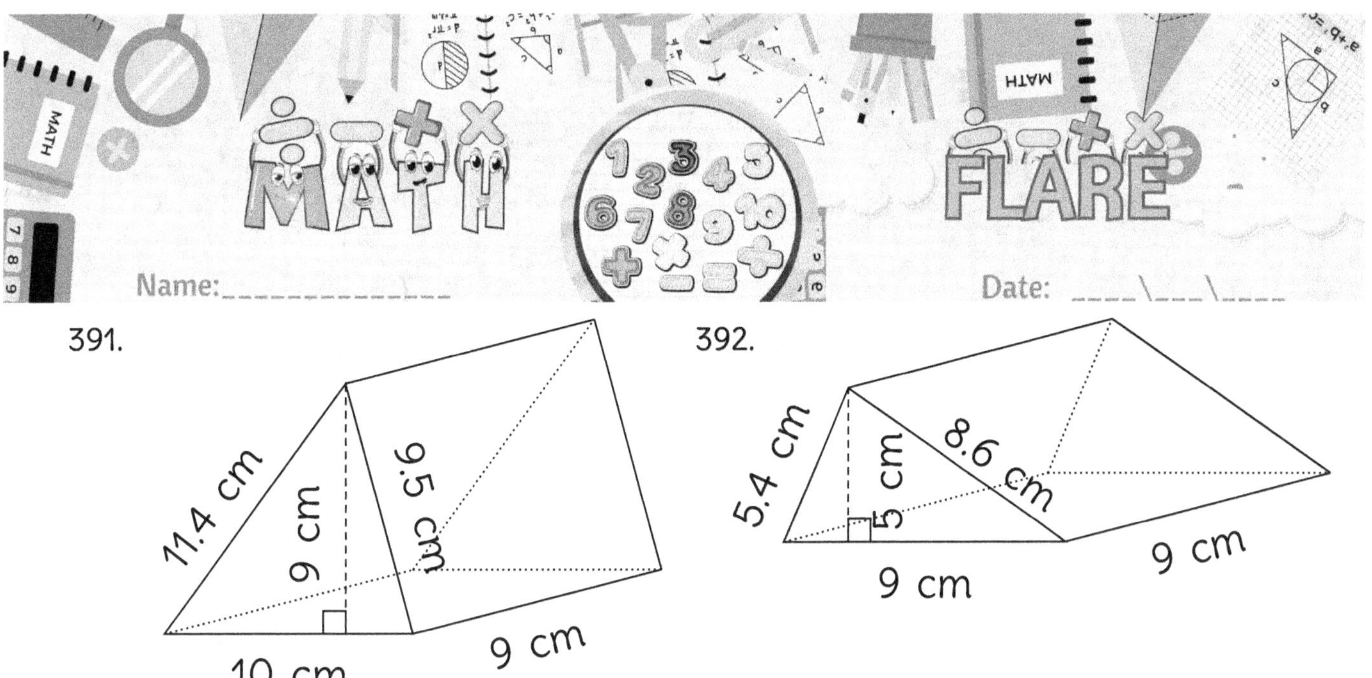

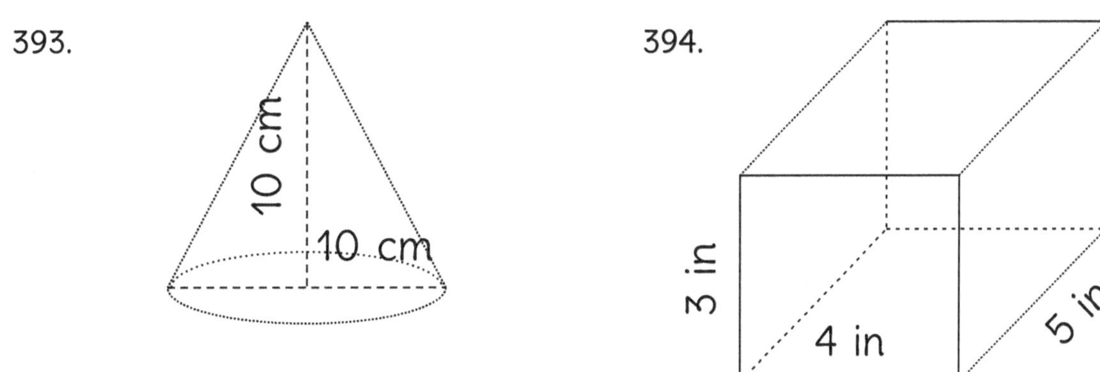

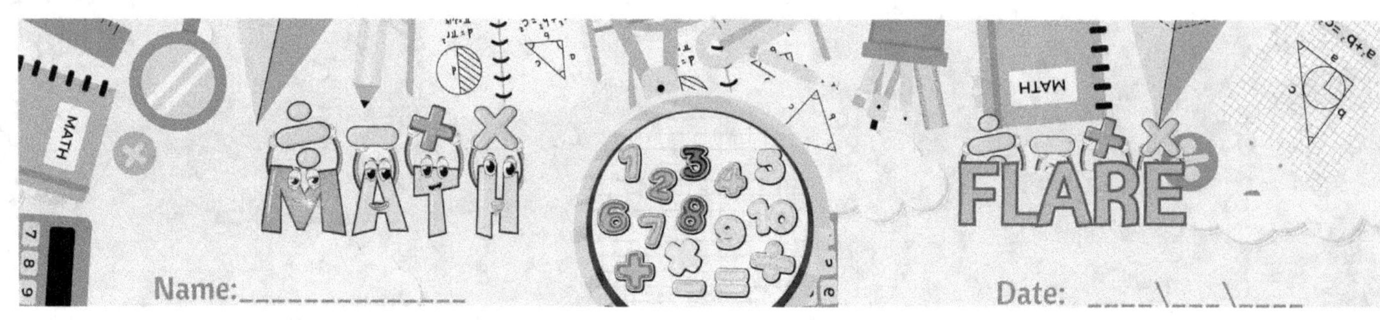

Circumference and Area

Calculate the circumference of each circle. Pi Value = 3.14

395.

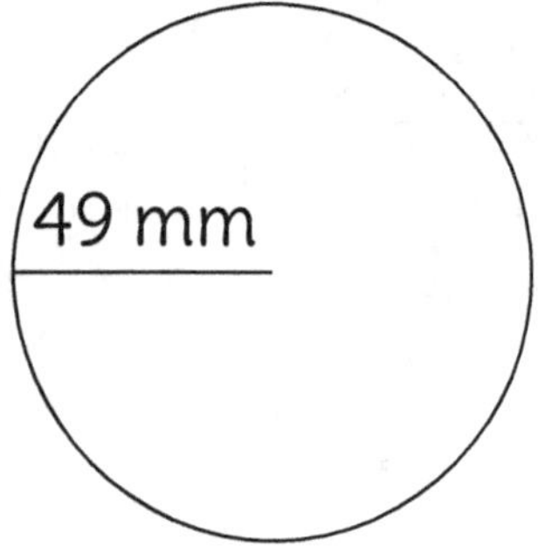

____
____

396.

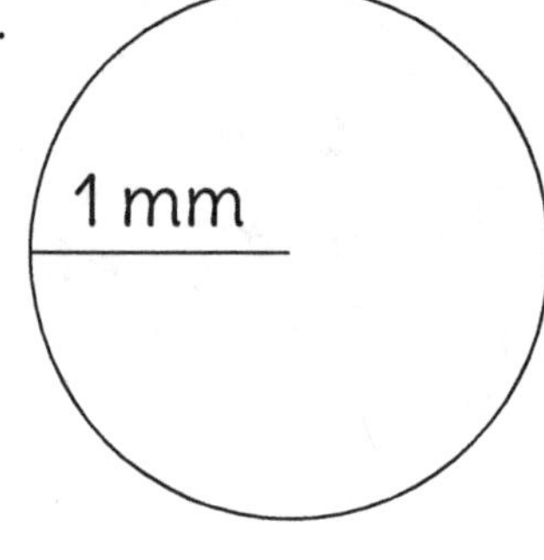

____
____

397.

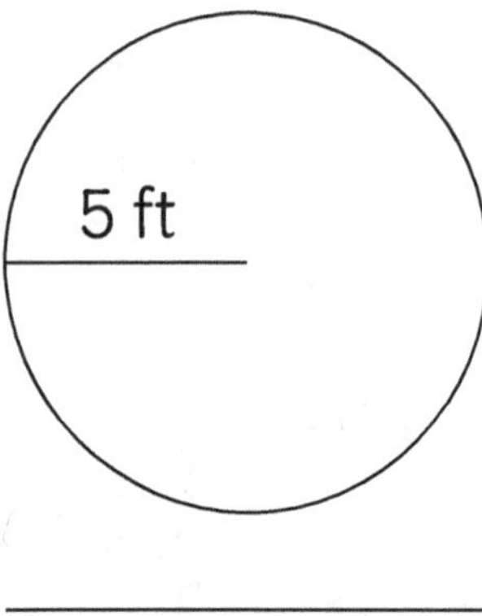

____
____

398.

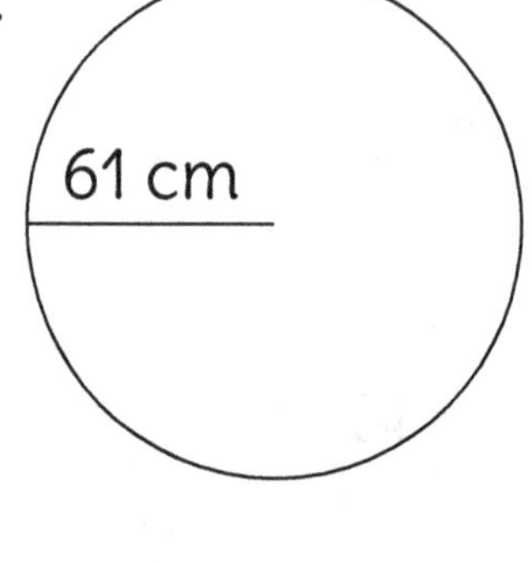

____
____

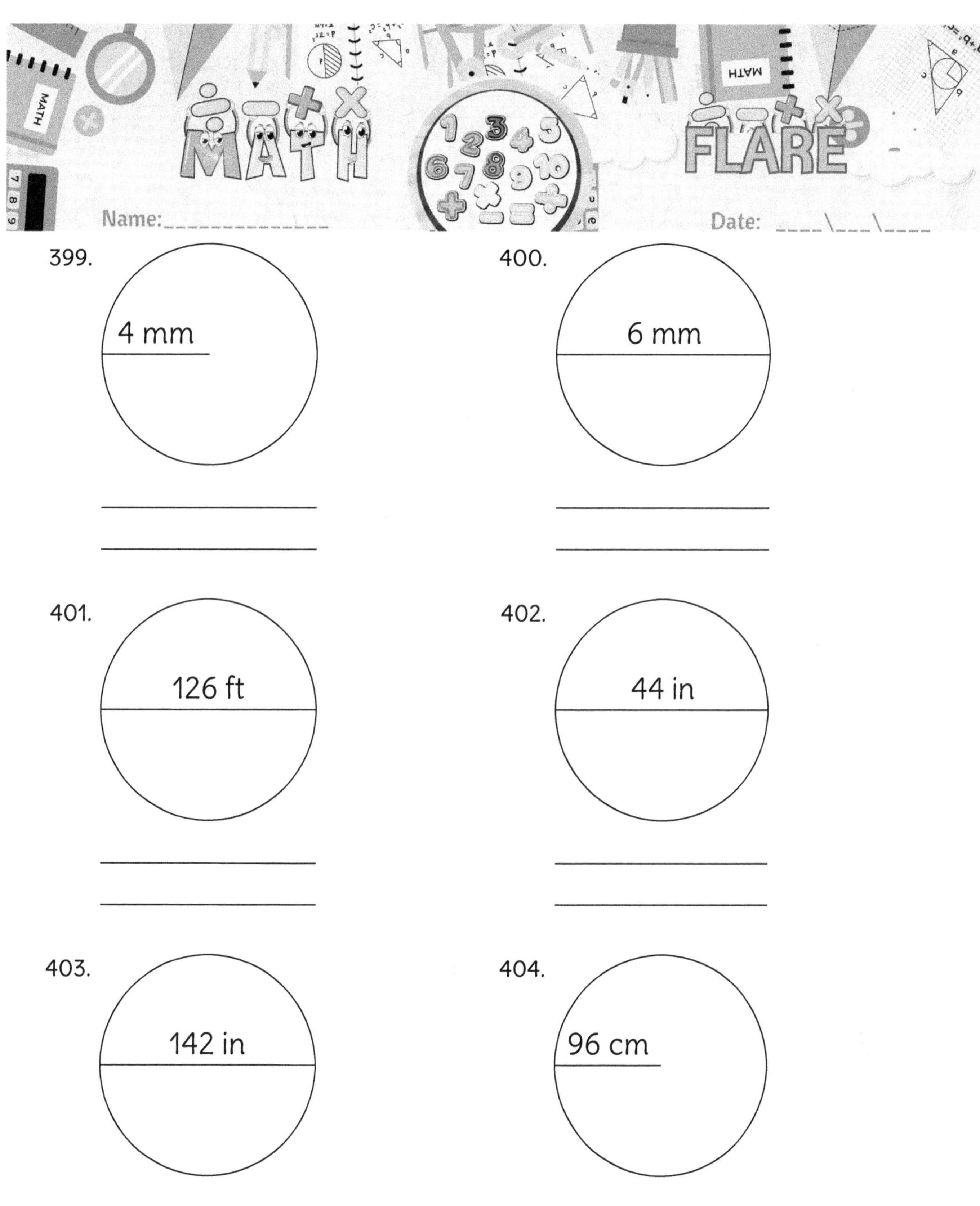
399.
4 mm

400.
6 mm

401.
126 ft

402.
44 in

403.
142 in

404.
96 cm

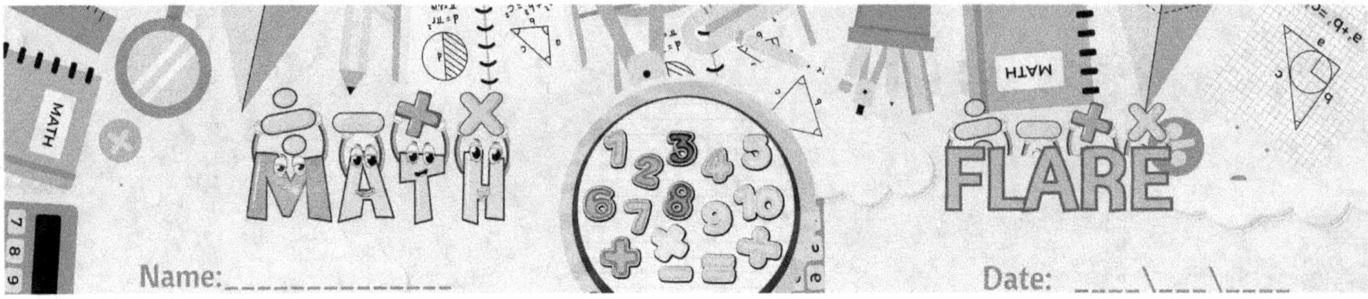

Name: _________________________   Date: ____________

405. 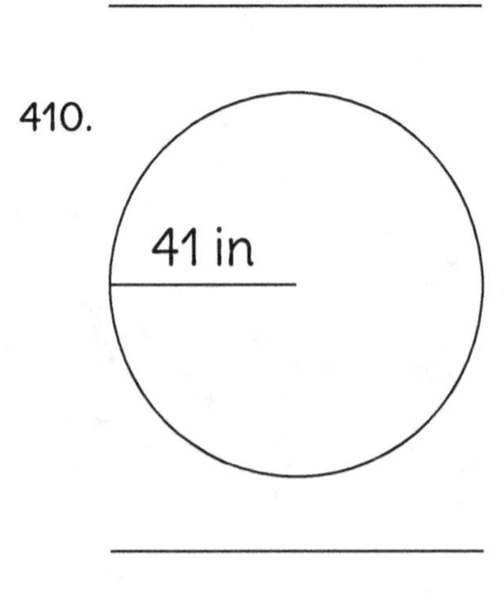

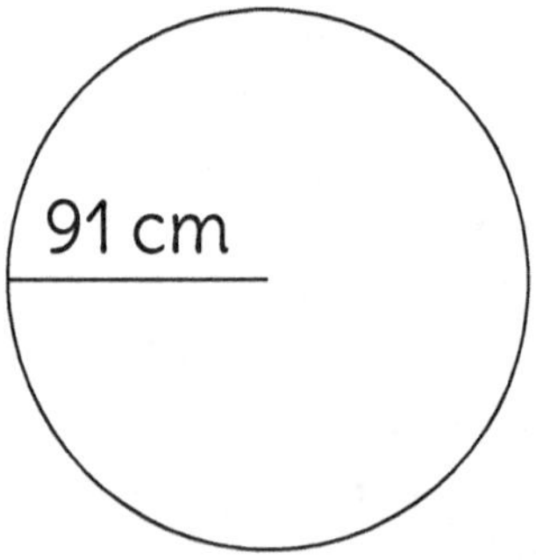

91 cm

____

406.

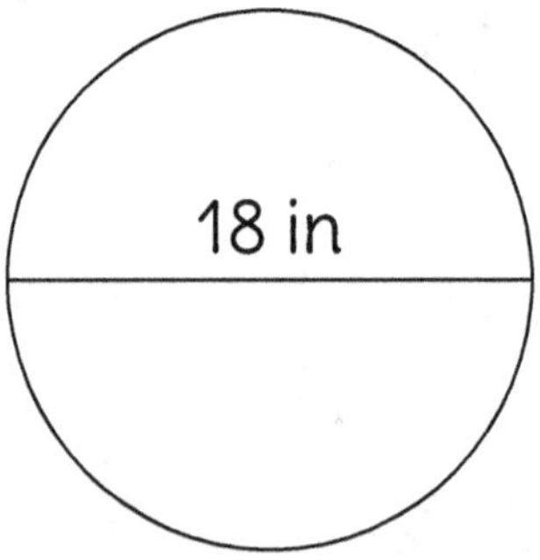

18 in

____

407.

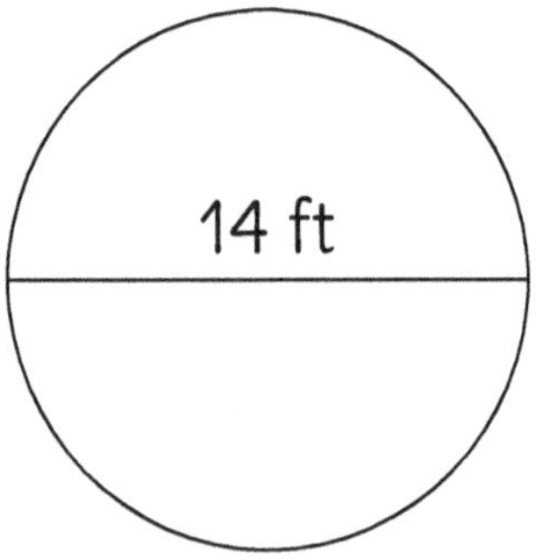

14 ft

____

408.

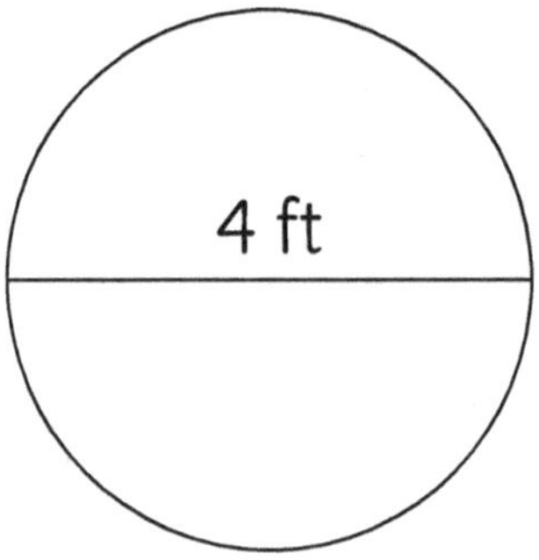

4 ft

____

409.

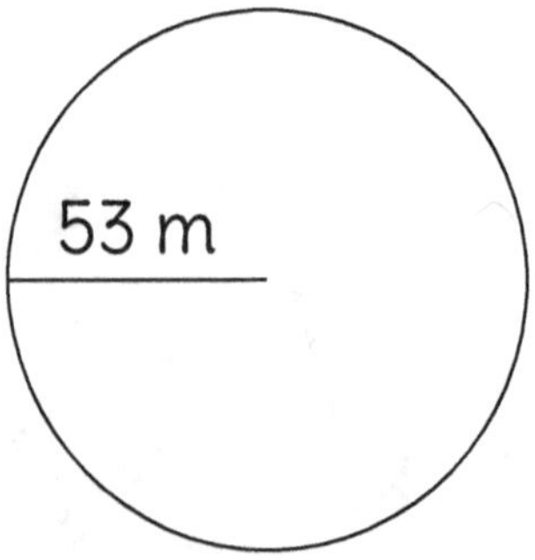

53 m

____

410.

41 in

____

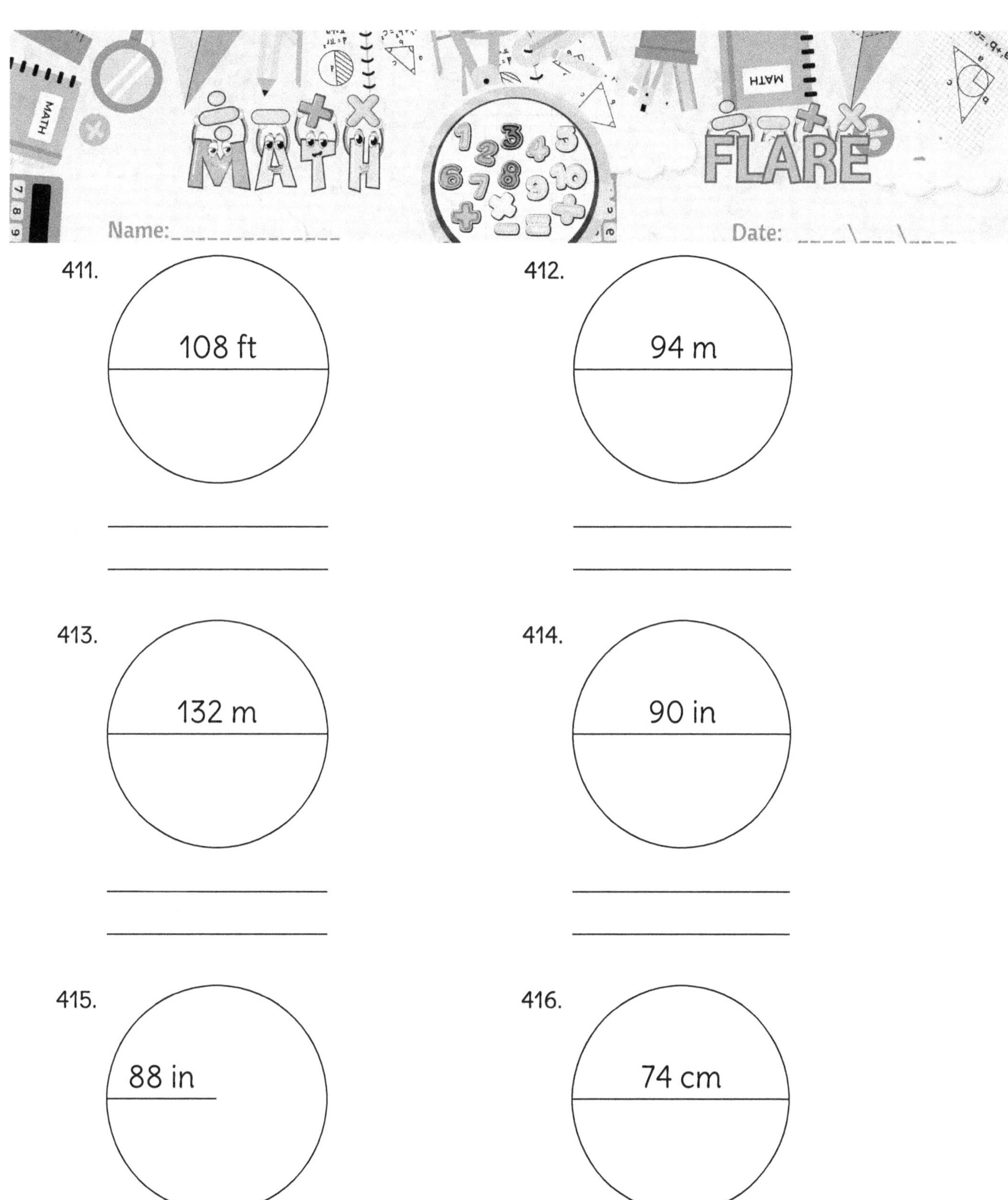
411.
108 ft
412.
94 m
413.
132 m
414.
90 in
415.
88 in
416.
74 cm

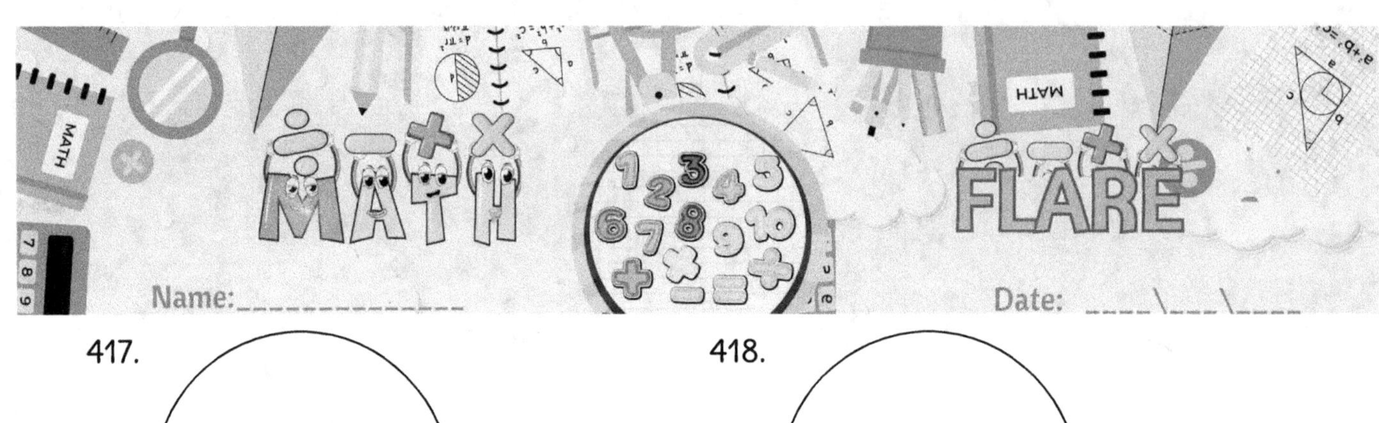

417.

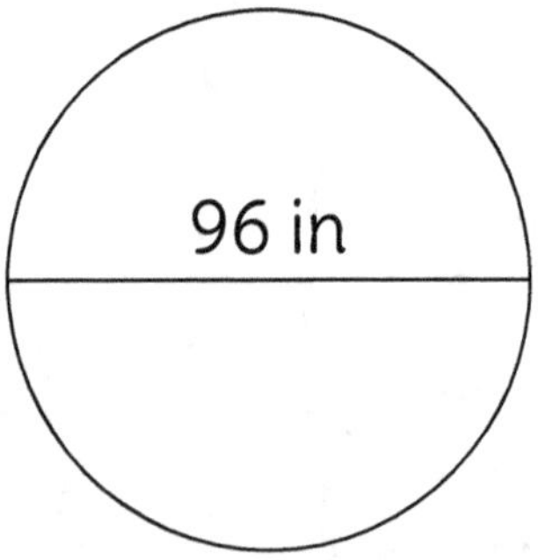

96 in

____

____

418.

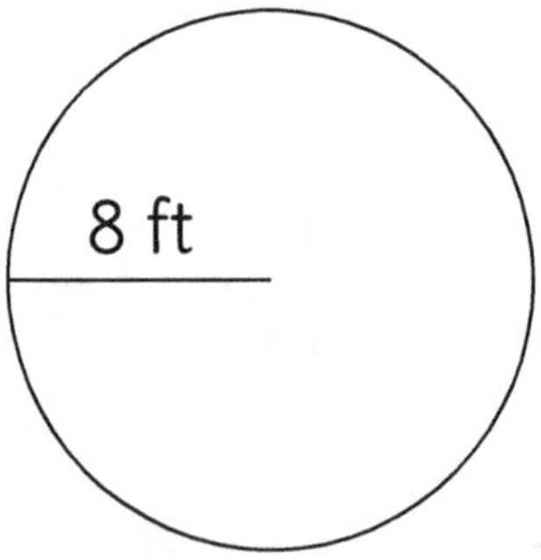

8 ft

____

____

419.

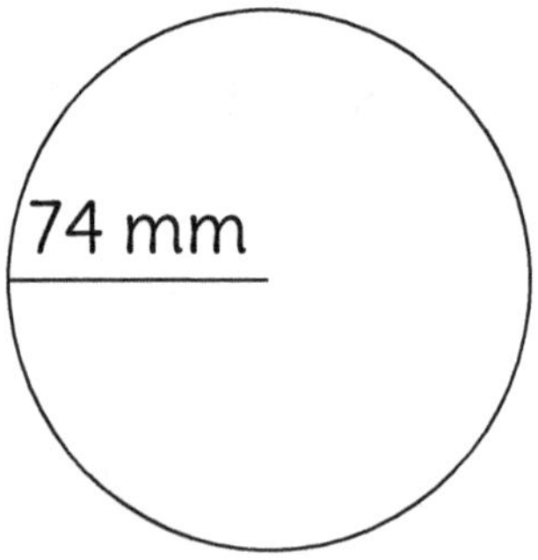

74 mm

____

____

420.

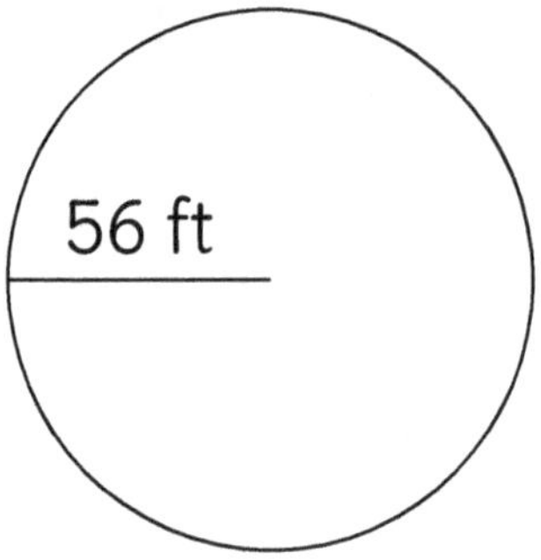

56 ft

____

____

421.

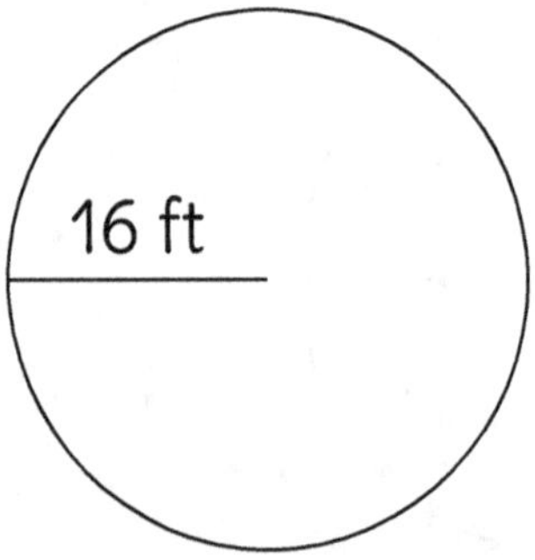

16 ft

____

____

422.

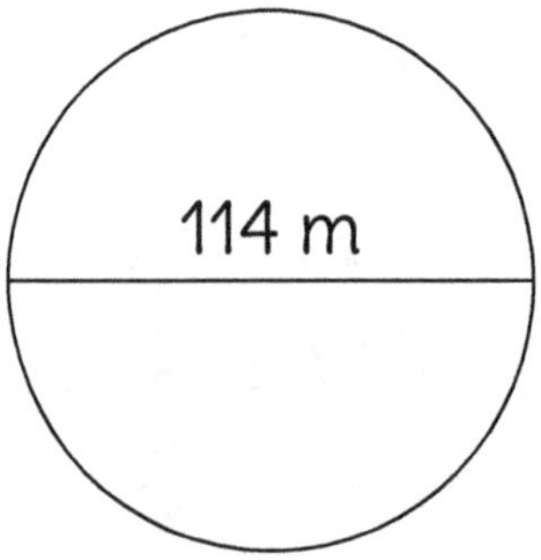

114 m

____

____

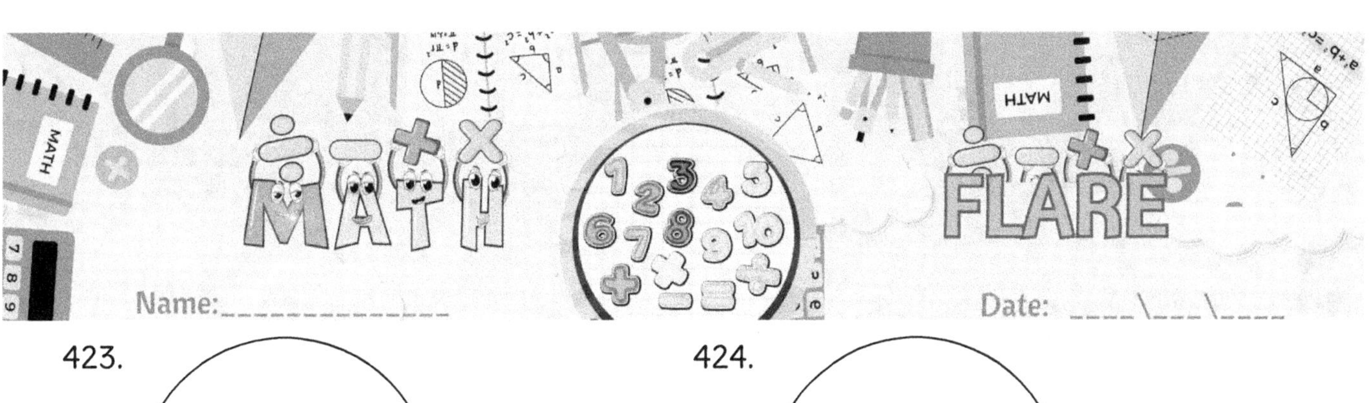

423.

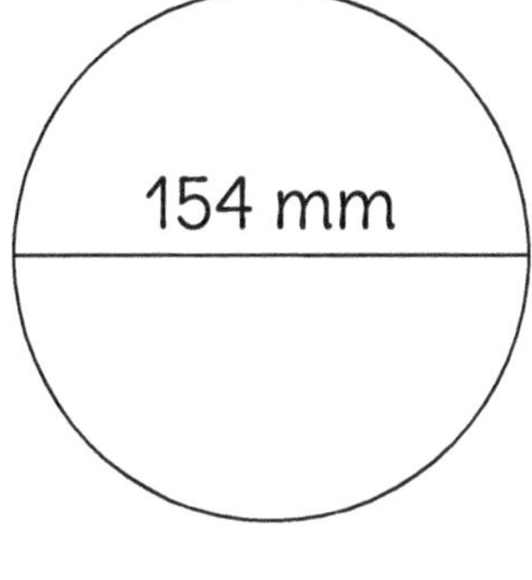

154 mm

424.

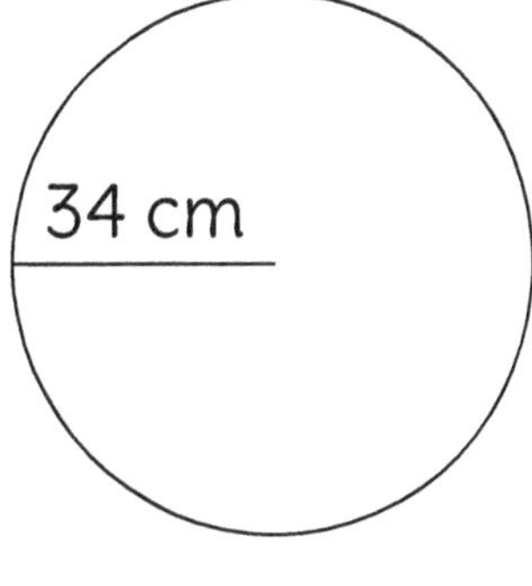

34 cm

425.

26 mm

426.

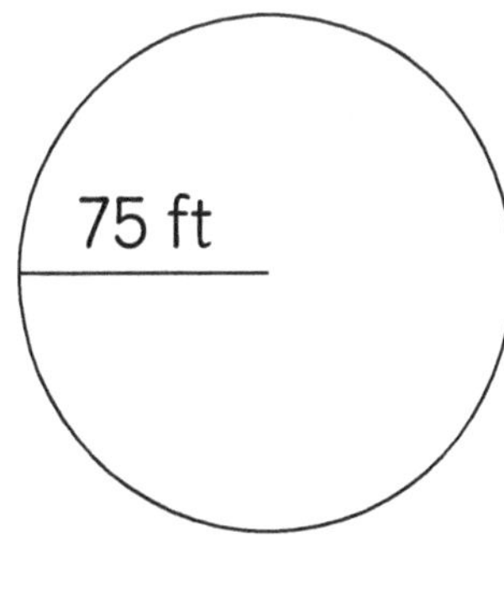

75 ft

427.

15 ft

428.

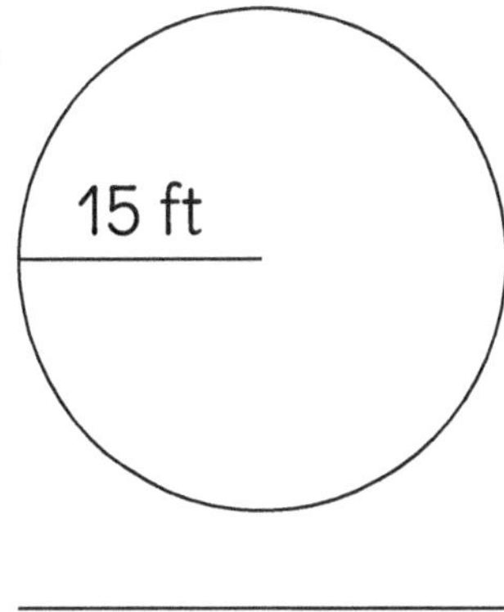

92 ft

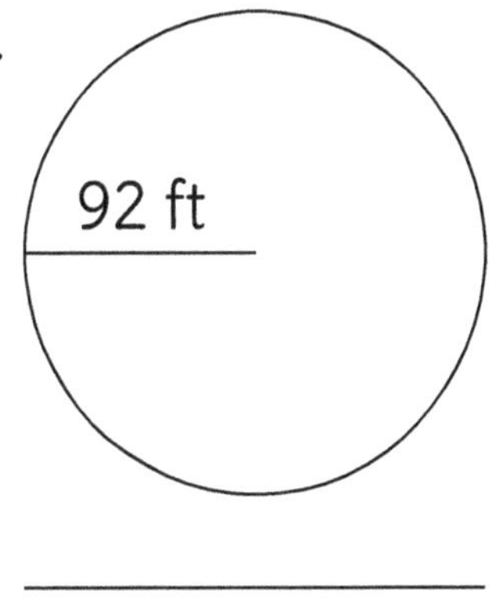

MathFlare - Units, Numerals, and Geometry

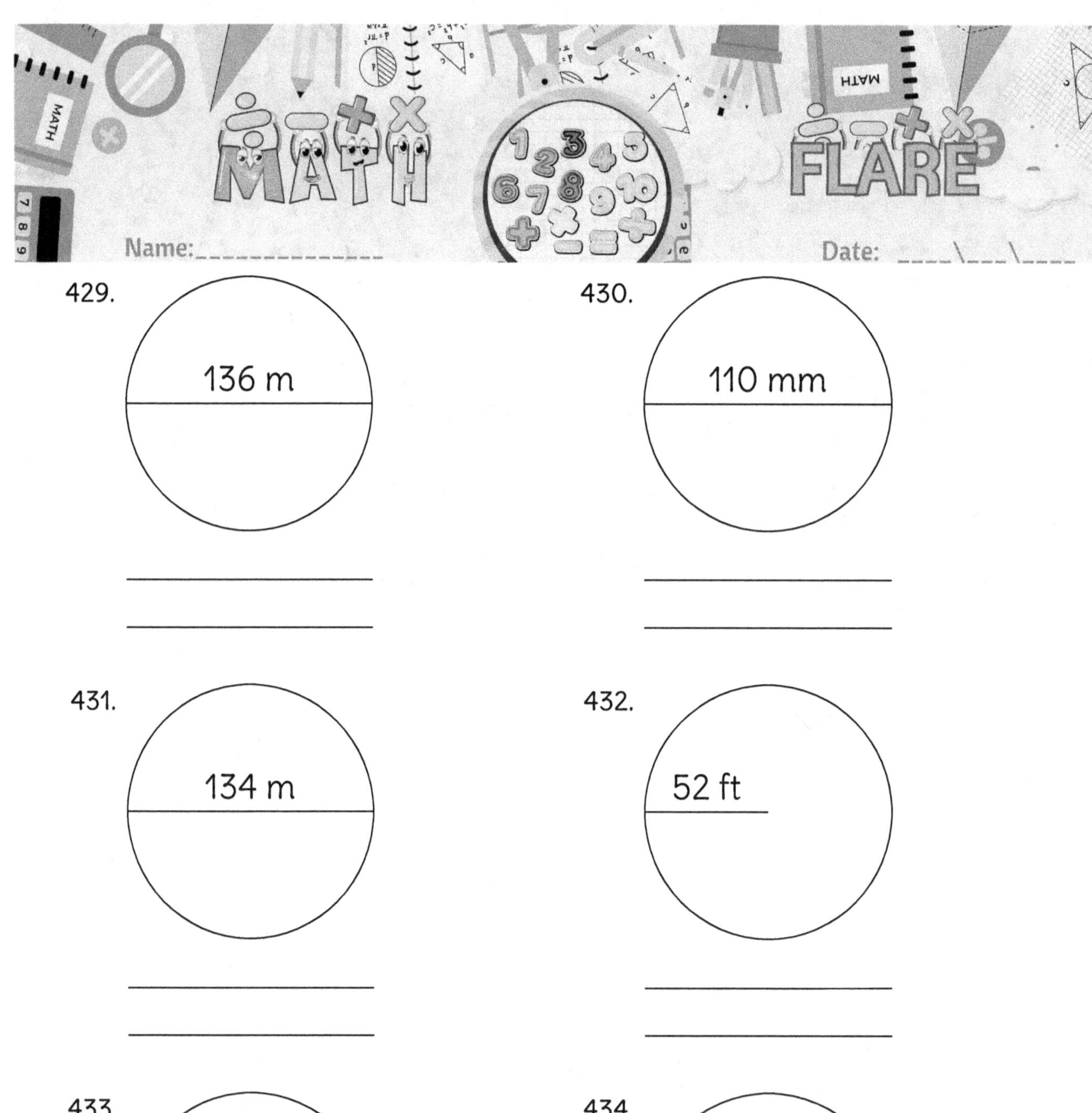

429. 136 m

430. 110 mm

431. 134 m

432. 52 ft

433. 30 m

434. 160 m

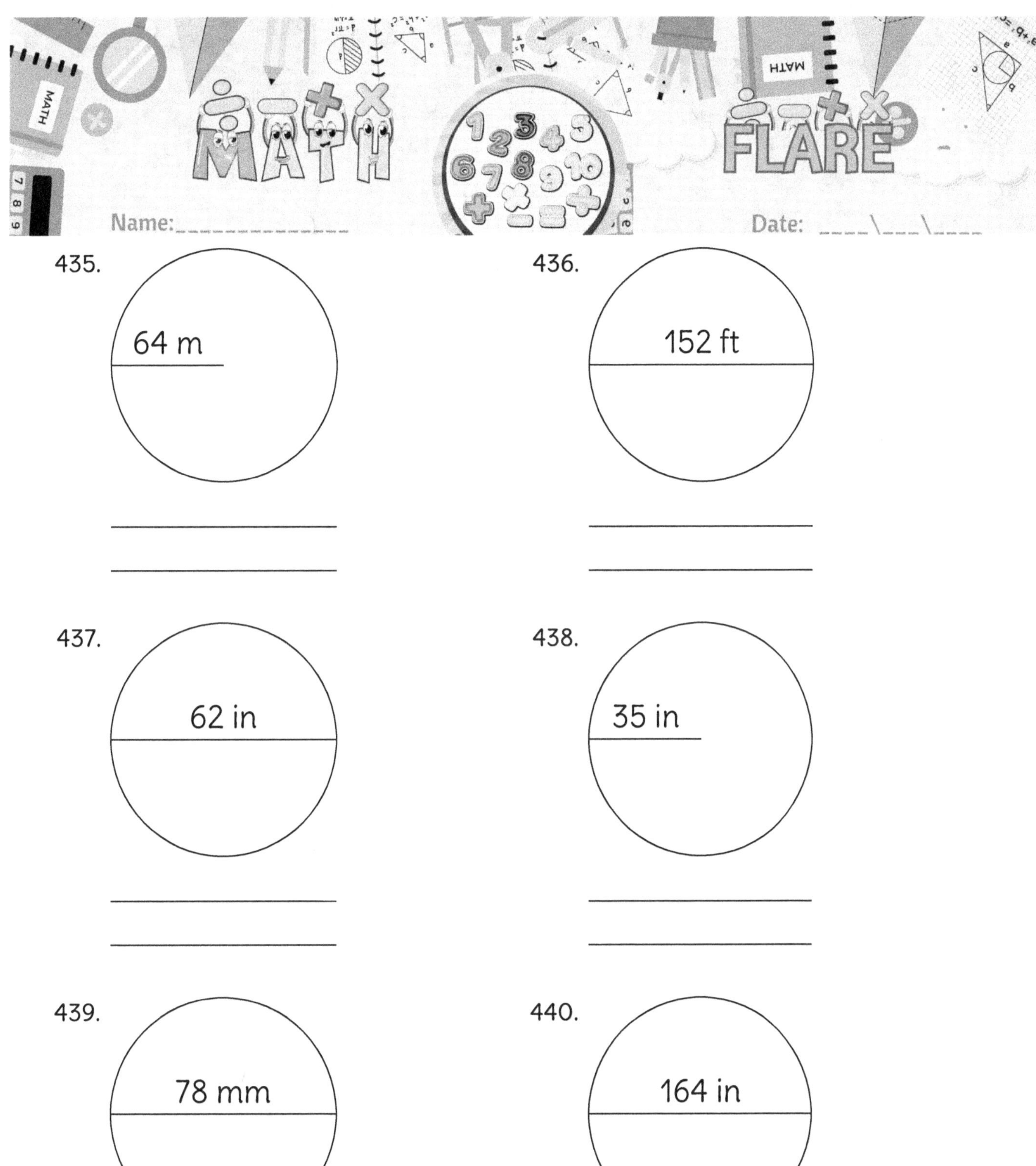

435. 64 m

436. 152 ft

437. 62 in

438. 35 in

439. 78 mm

440. 164 in

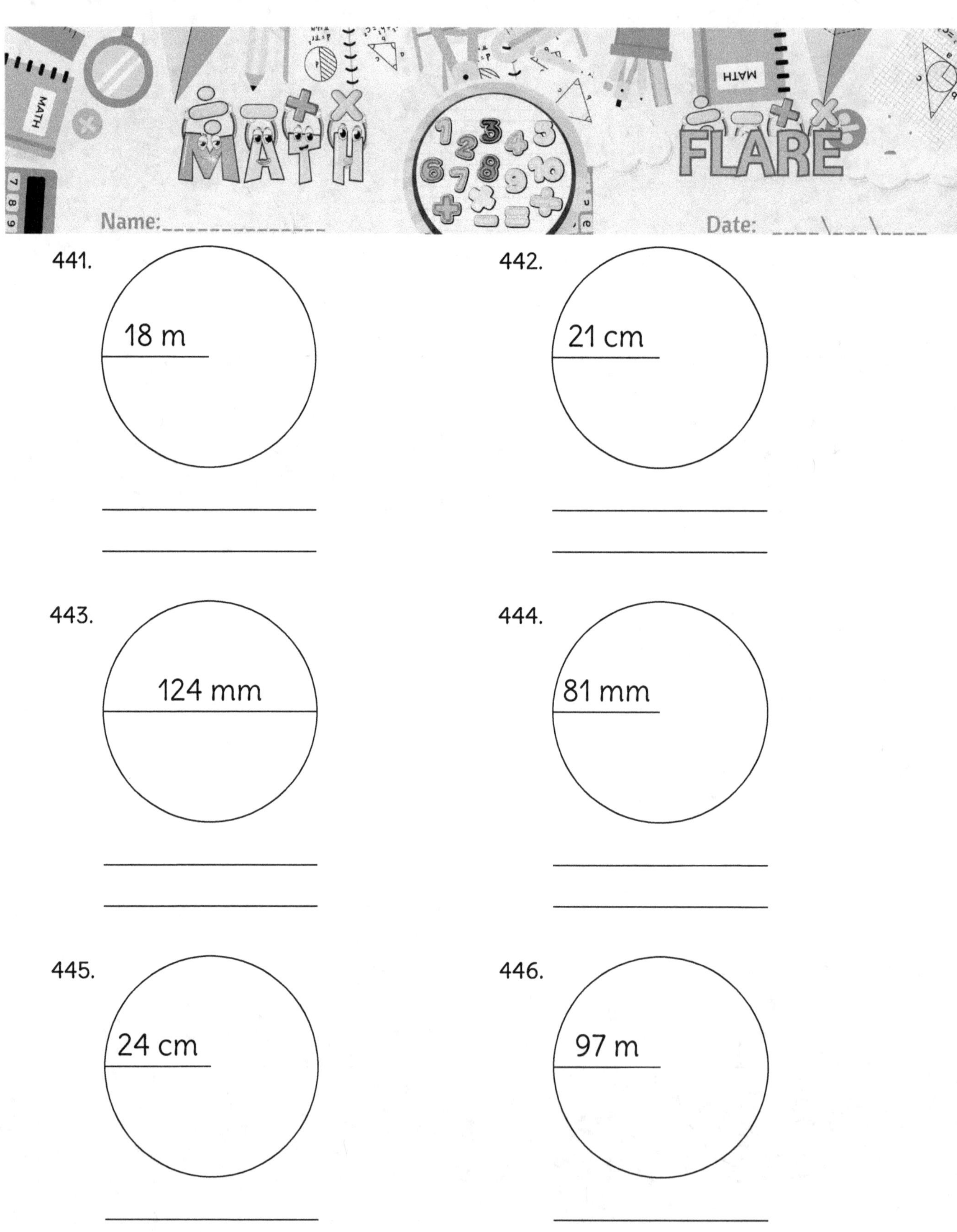

441.
18 m
442.
21 cm
443.
124 mm
444.
81 mm
445.
24 cm
446.
97 m

ANSWERS

Page 1: Roman Numerals

1. 7	2. VI	3. XXXVI
4. 31	5. CCCXXXIX	6. LXXI
7. LXVIII	8. LXXXVII	9. 1
10. LXXIII	11. 487	12. 465
13. 148	14. 311	15. 2
16. 47	17. 4	18. 63
19. 3	20. XXVII	21. 246
22. LVIII	23. CXCVII	24. 304
25. IX	26. 90	27. CDLXXIII
28. XLIX	29. 480	30. LXXIX
31. LVII	32. 72	33. XCIX
34. 112	35. CCXXXVII	36. CCCXCV
37. 358	38. 19	39. CCLXXIII
40. CCXVII	41. XXXIX	42. CDIX
43. 248	44. X	45. 227
46. CCCLXXI	47. CCV	48. 55
49. 28	50. LXXX	51. 83
52. 54	53. 29	54. 436
55. 74	56. 23	57. 18

58. 284	59. LXV	60. CCLVI
61. 41	62. CXXX	63. CCCXXXI
64. 257	65. 56	66. 14
67. 325	68. CCX	69. CXVII
70. CDXXXIX	71. 92	72. 415
73. 472	74. 272	75. 149
76. VIII	77. CCI	78. CCXCII
79. 45	80. 5	81. CLXXVIII
82. XXXIII	83. 485	84. CCLXXXIX
85. CCCXLV	86. 308	87. 270
88. LIII	89. 452	90. 89
91. 11	92. 338	93. LXXXI
94. 211	95. CDXLIX	96. CDXL
97. CDLXII	98. XIII	99. XXI
100. CDIII	101. 319	102. CCXXIII
103. 320	104. XXIV	105. 490
106. 354	107. 44	108. 498
109. 12	110. CDLXXXVIII	111. CDXXIX
112. CCCXXVIII	113. CCLVIII	114. 82
115. 307	116. CLXVI	117. LII
118. 212	119. CCLXVIII	120. 323

121. 137	122. CCXCV	123. LXXVI
124. CDLIV	125. 324	126. 66
127. 69	128. 26	129. 438
130. 84	131. XLII	132. 441
133. 352	134. CDXCII	135. CCCX
136. CLII	137. 240	138. XCV
139. 333	140. 277	141. 115
142. CDLVI	143. 25	144. CCCLXXXI
145. 469	146. CDLXXXI	147. 77
148. 75	149. 193	150. CCLX
151. 305	152. CCCLXXIX	153. CCCLXXV
154. CCXIII		

Page 12: Metric Conversion

155. 1.905	156. 11.278	157. 1.930	158. 25.298	159. 1.524
160. 9.449	161. 26.213	162. 27.432	163. 25.603	164. 0.279
165. 2.515	166. 1.854	167. 1.245	168. 3.962	169. 19.202
170. 8.839	171. 1.499	172. 2.337	173. 0.254	174. 1.702
175. 2.311	176. 0.457	177. 21.641	178. 11.278	179. 11.278
180. 0.635	181. 2.210	182. 0.559	183. 0.406	184. 11.278
185. 7.620	186. 1.803	187. 1.448	188. 1.549	189. 28.042
190. 1.499	191. 0.660	192. 12.497	193. 5.486	194. 2.337

195. 15.240   196. 0.914   197. 7.620   198. 8.839   199. 1.575

200. 1.549   201. 1.422   202. 0.889   203. 21.031   204. 2.159

205. 15.240   206. 8.839   207. 2.134   208. 2.413   209. 1.626

210. 20.422   211. 19.812   212. 14.935   213. 1.422   214. 13.716

215. 1.092   216. 22.250   217. 2.134   218. 1.422   219. 2.159

220. 11.582   221. 7.620   222. 2.210   223. 6.096   224. 0.356

Page 16: Metric Weights and Measures

225. 1,400   226. 0.000028   227. 0.084

228. 0.017   229. 0.000027   230. 6,500

231. 9,200,000   232. 52,000   233. 0.000075

234. 0.075   235. 68,000   236. 6,200,000

237. 31,000   238. 8,700,000   239. 95,000,000

240. 86,000,000   241. 61,000   242. 97,000

243. 35,000   244. 93,000   245. 76,000,000

246. 84,000,000   247. 72,000   248. 0.059

249. 0.000076   250. 0.00052   251. 0.068

252. 43,000   253. 34,000   254. 0.045

255. 68,000   256. 25,000   257. 65,000

258. 0.081   259. 31,000   260. 0.044

261. 7,600,000   262. 7,800   263. 0.98

264. 7,400,000   265. 23,000,000   266. 0.073

267. 7,900,000

268. 0.000076

269. 80,000,000

270. 0.31

271. 63,000

272. 69,000

273. 0.090

274. 0.050

275. 0.063

276. 0.089

Page 19: Area and Perimeter: Rectangles and Triangles

277. P=24 A=24.5

278. P=21 A=17.5

279. P=53 A=119

280. P=42 A=84.87

281. P=39 A=73.18

282. P=54 A=182

283. P=34 A=72

284. P=48 A=143

285. P=24 A=35

286. P=34 A=50

287. P=27 A=35.07

288. P=30 A=56

289. P=26 A=32.24

290. P=33 A=52.42

291. P=58 A=208

292. P=36 A=62.35

293. P=42 A=110

294. P=44 A=120

295. P=41 A=71.5

296. P=26 A=32.24

297. P=35 A=54.9

298. P=28 A=31.5

299. P=42 A=84.84

300. P=38 A=90

301. P=36 A=54

302. P=53 A=119

303. P=48 A=110.88

304. P=54 A=180

305. P=27 A=32

306. P=26 A=42

307. P=27 A=31.5

308. P=48 A=144

309. P=34 A=54.55

310. P=22 A=21

311. P=21 A=17.5

312. P=32 A=45.24

313. P=21 A=21.22

314. P=27 A=35.07

315. P=22 A=21

316. P=48 A=110.85

317. P=60 A=153

318. P=24 A=27.71

319. P=52 A=165

320. P=24 A=24.5

321. P=29 A=36

322. P=25 A=28

323. P=48 A=143

324. P=35 A=58.68

325. P=30 A=43.3   326. P=19 A=15   327. P=32 A=49

328. P=30 A=56   329. P=34 A=72   330. P=41 A=76.78

331. P=36 A=55   332. P=37 A=64.79   333. P=41 A=70

334. P=40 A=96

Page 34: Volume and Surface Area

335. V=382 in³ in³ SA=254 in² in²

336. V=360 in³ in³ SA=348.0 in² in²

337. V=269.39 cm³ cm³ SA=231 cm² cm²

338. V=6.28 ft³ ft³ SA=19 ft² ft²

339. V=65 in³ in³ SA=79 in² in²

340. V=7 in³ in³ SA=23 in² in²

341. V=50.27 in³ in³ SA=75 in² in²

342. V=216 cm³ cm³ SA=216 cm² cm²

343. V=78.54 cm³ cm³ SA=102 cm² cm²

344. V=60 cm³ cm³ SA=104 cm² cm²

345. V=105 ft³ ft³ SA=148.0 ft² ft²

346. V=80 in³ in³ SA=112 in² in²

347. V=125 in³ in³ SA=150 in² in²

348. V=117.81 ft³ ft³ SA=134 ft² ft²

349. V=9.42 ft³ ft³ SA=25 ft² ft²

350. V=120 cm³ cm³ SA=148 cm² cm²

351. V=62 cm³ cm³ SA=107.5 cm² cm²

352. V=100 cm³ cm³ SA=130 cm² cm²

353. V=64 in³ in³ SA=106 in² in²

354. V=60 in³ in³ SA=94 in² in²

355. V=72 ft³ ft³ SA=123.6 ft² ft²

356. V=252 cm³ cm³ SA=240 cm² cm²

357. V=12 in³ in³ SA=32 in² in²

358. V=75 ft³ ft³ SA=110 ft² ft²

359. V=103 ft³ ft³ SA=134 ft² ft²

360. V=9 ft³ ft³ SA=27 ft² ft²

361. V=378 ft³ ft³ SA=318 ft² ft²

362. V=209 cm³ cm³ SA=227 cm² cm²

363. V=40 ft³ ft³ SA=79.2 ft² ft²

364. V=94 ft³ ft³ SA=127 ft² ft²

365. V=80 ft³ ft³ SA=112 ft² ft²

366. V=137.44 cm³ cm³ SA=149 cm² cm²

367. V=201.06 cm³ cm³ SA=201 cm² cm²

368. V=100 cm³ cm³ SA=130 cm² cm²

369. V=294 cm³ cm³ SA=266 cm² cm²

370. V=50 cm³ cm³ SA=93.4 cm² cm²

371. V=32 in³ in³ SA=70.8 in² in²

372. V=141.37 ft³ ft³ SA=151 ft² ft²

373. V=5 in³ in³ SA=19 in² in²

374. V=252 in³ in³ SA=240 in² in²

375. V=27 in³ in³ SA=54 in² in²

376. V=113.10 in³ in³ SA=132 in² in²

377. V=441 ft³ ft³ SA=350 ft² ft²

378. V=9 ft³ ft³ SA=31.8 ft² ft²

379. V=301.59 cm³ cm³ SA=251 cm² cm²

380. V=80 in³ in³ SA=112 in² in²

381. V=576 in³ in³ SA=416 in² in²

382. V=125 in³ in³ SA=150 in² in²

383. V=12 ft³ ft³ SA=32 ft² ft²

384. V=336 ft³ ft³ SA=292 ft² ft²

385. V=560 ft³ ft³ SA=412 ft² ft²

386. V=6 in³ in³ SA=23.2 in² in²

387. V=140 ft³ ft³ SA=184.0 ft² ft²

388. V=120 in³ in³ SA=148 in² in²

389. V=392 in³ in³ SA=322 in² in²

390. V=210 cm³ cm³ SA=214 cm² cm²

391. V=405 cm³ cm³ SA=368.1 cm² cm²

392. V=202 cm³ cm³ SA=252.0 cm² cm²

393. V=262 cm³ cm³ SA=254 cm² cm²

394. V=60 in³ in³ SA=94 in² in²

Page 49: Circumference and Area

395. C=307.72 mm A=7,539.14 mm²

396. C=6.28 mm A=3.14 mm²

397. C=31.40 ft A=78.50 ft²

398. C=383.08 cm A=11,683.94 cm²

399. C=25.12 mm A=50.24 mm²

400. C=18.84 mm A=28.26 mm²

401. C=395.64 ft A=12,462.66 ft²

402. C=138.16 in A=1,519.76 in²

403. C=445.88 in A=15,828.74 in²

404. C=602.88 cm A=28,938.24 cm²

405. C=571.48 cm A=26,002.34 cm²

406. C=56.52 in A=254.34 in²

407. C=43.96 ft A=153.86 ft²

408. C=12.56 ft A=12.56 ft²

409. C=332.84 m A=8,820.26 m²

410. C=257.48 in A=5,278.34 in²

411. C=339.12 ft A=9,156.24 ft²

412. C=295.16 m A=6,936.26 m²

413. C=414.48 m A=13,677.84 m²

414. C=282.60 in A=6,358.50 in²

415. C=552.64 in A=24,316.16 in²

416. C=232.36 cm A=4,298.66 cm²

417. C=301.44 in A=7,234.56 in²

418. C=50.24 ft A=200.96 ft²

419. C=464.72 mm A=17,194.64 mm²

420. C=351.68 ft A=9,847.04 ft²

421. C=100.48 ft A=803.84 ft²

422. C=357.96 m A=10,201.86 m²

423. C=483.56 mm A=18,617.06 mm²

424. C=213.52 cm A=3,629.84 cm²

425. C=81.64 mm A=530.66 mm²

426. C=471.00 ft A=17,662.50 ft²

427. C=94.20 ft A=706.50 ft²

428. C=577.76 ft A=26,576.96 ft²

429. C=427.04 m A=14,519.36 m²

430. C=345.40 mm A=9,498.50 mm²

431. C=420.76 m A=14,095.46 m²

432. C=326.56 ft A=8,490.56 ft²

433. C=188.40 m A=2,826.00 m²

434. C=502.40 m A=20,096.00 m²

435. C=401.92 m A=12,861.44 m²

436. C=477.28 ft A=18,136.64 ft²

437. C=194.68 in A=3,017.54 in²

438. C=219.80 in A=3,846.50 in²

439. C=244.92 mm A=4,775.94 mm²

440. C=514.96 in A=21,113.36 in²

441. C=113.04 m A=1,017.36 m²

442. C=131.88 cm A=1,384.74 cm²

443. C=389.36 mm A=12,070.16 mm²

444. C=508.68 mm A=20,601.54 mm²

445. C=150.72 cm A=1,808.64 cm²

446. C=609.16 m A=29,544.26 m²

www.ingramcontent.com/pod-product-compliance
Lightning Source LLC
Chambersburg PA
CBHW081355160726

48000CB00010B/3361